# MARKETSHOCK

More Than Fifty Insiders Tell
How to Survive and Profit
from Today's Global
Financial Revolution

## MARK FADIMAN

JOHN WILEY & SONS, INC.

New York  •  Chichester  •  Brisbane  •  Toronto  •  Singapore

*Twilight of Sovereignty* excerpt reprinted with the permission of Scribner's, an imprint of Simon & Schuster. Copyright © 1992, Walter B. Wriston.

The author acknowledges permission to draw on portions of several interviews conducted by Larry Chambers and Chuck Epstein. Brief summaries of a few interviews by this book's author were previously published in *Financial Planning On Wall Street*. Part of the Charles Fahy interview appeared in a different form in *FPWS*.

*Library of Congress Cataloging-in-Publication Data:*

Fadiman, Mark.
    Marketshock : more than fifty insiders tell how to survive and
profit from today's global financial revolution / Mark Fadiman.
      p.  cm.
    ISBN 0-471-59909-3
    1. Program trading (Securities)  2. Stockbrokers—United States—
Interviews.  3. Financial services industry.  4. Speculation.
5. Twenty-first century—Forecasts.  I. Title.  II. Title: Market
shock.
HG4515.5.F33   1994
332.6—dc20                    94-27134

*To*
CINDY

"A wise and frugal Government, which shall restrain men from injuring one another, shall leave them otherwise free to regulate their own pursuits of industry and improvement."

Thomas Jefferson<br>First Inaugural Address, 1801

# FOREWORD

Few investors can feel sanguine about the prospect of massive, worldwide market collapses flattening their portfolios and hopes alike. Trouble is, where do you find a suitable remedy? Grabbing the latest financial fad to boost returns isn't the answer. All too often that results only in throwing good money after bad.

Most might find their performance improves when they understand the broader trends that lie behind market surges and shocks. That is what Mark Fadiman does here with rare skill. Fadiman's approach is deceptively simple but shrewd. He has interviewed more than 50 professionals who make—and break—markets in both the United States and abroad. By distilling their thoughts and analyzing their conclusions, Fadiman helps expose the widening array of risks that investors face.

Fadiman skillfully traces a little-understood but critical modern phenomenon: the ongoing collision of technology and regulation that all too often gives rise to market volatility. This is material that investors ignore at their own peril. We can be thankful that Fadiman has used his Rolodex so diligently and done much of our legwork for us. His vignettes help us to understand financial markets as they really are, not as many who work in—or report on—finance would have the public believe they are.

Fadiman goes to the core of the problem facing today's investors. Investing for the long haul probably won't work if you need to get your money out at one particular time. That date—three, five, or even ten years hence—when you desperately want funds for retirement, to pay off the mortgage, or send a child or grandchild to college—may coincide with some unforeseen marketshock.

Investing for the long haul becomes increasingly hazardous when the time horizon for professional money managers rarely stretches beyond their next performance review. And the pressure to perform among these professionals will rise until the inevitable blood bath takes place on Wall Street itself.

Excessive capacity breeds immoderate competition and raises toleration levels for risk to dangerous heights. All that competition will make its own contribution to whatever marketshocks are in store for us. Few in the public and surprisingly few in the media realize how much the financial industry has changed. As I outlined in my own book, *Bear Trap: Why Wall Street Doesn't Work*, three major and two minor forces intertwine and react against each other and then produce more change. The three major ones are technology, globalization, and deregulation. The minor ones are ethics and taxation. By tracing these forces over the past 30 years, you begin to see a Wall Street and a financial services industry business that is far different from what the public perceives or what the media mostly portray. Firms in the investment business have quietly shifted their strategies. No longer are they content with their traditional role of acting as an agent or middleman in the raising of capital and the distributing of shares and bonds for others.

That's a role with scant prospect for growth. Worse, it's not a business likely to pay the fat bonuses most Wall Streeters expect to pocket. In their pursuit of greater profits, Wall Street firms have increasingly switched from agent to principal, betting their own funds. No question, in recent times this change of strategy has helped these firms partially to reverse the long downward pressure on their margins, but not without adding risk—for themselves and for everyone participating in the financial markets.

Again, there are no guarantees when Wall Street bets its own money.

Money now moves at lightning speed around the globe in a bevy of increasingly exotic and perilous financial instruments. Currencies, interest rates, commodities, stocks, and bonds are all now intertwined and react against each other. Complexity has replaced simplicity in investing, though you wouldn't know it from listening to many market commentators.

Consider just one aspect of this. Technology in the form of cheap communications and even cheaper computing power is starting to make a mockery of the simple idea of stock or bond selection. We're seeing the emergence of two quite distinct approaches to investing—one by the general public and the other by professional investors.

For the most part, individuals still trade stocks and bonds the old-fashioned way, one at a time. Professionals increasingly trade in huge blocks, whole portfolios, or whole regions of the world at a time. Often all that's involved are a few computer keystrokes made in reaction to the latest news flash from some distant region of the globe. No matter that the news may be erroneous or that mature reflection will take the sting out of what were perceived to be bad tidings, the motto of a growing number of professionals is, React first, think later.

Can average investors defend themselves against such behavior? In this insightful and comprehensive overview, Fadiman attempts to show some of the emerging techniques that could be used to defend customers against marketshock. His scheme divides up investment strategies, worldwide, into Big Money, New Money, and Hot Money. The simplicity of his categories allows readers to make sense of financial trends they may well not have been aware of before. His perception of a new kind of diversification—built around strategies, not instruments—applies the knowledgeable financial analysis to our modern financial industry that is sorely lacking among his peers.

Of course none of this is a panacea. As I pointed out in *Bear Trap*, it's also probably true that no amount of diversification or financial hedging can profitably offset a rolling, worldwide, or even regional marketshock. Still, as Fadiman suggests, more rational regulation—combined with new investment techniques and the use of judicious leverage and hedging—may at least begin to even the odds private investors face.

Even those who disagree with Fadiman's analysis will come away with a better idea of the realities of the modern financial industry as well as the furious, intricate debates between financial regulators and investment pros around the world. The financial industry of the 21st century will be far different from that of the 20th. Those who do not take the time to understand these differences will be operating under tremendous disadvantages. *MarketShock* is an investment primer for the 21st century.

PAUL GIBSON
Former *Forbes* senior editor
Author, *Bear Trap: Why Wall Street Doesn't Work*

# Acknowledgments

This book is international in scope but aimed at domestic investors who may not understand global opportunities and perils. As America's largest generation, its baby boomers, plan for old age, educated investing becomes critical. I hope this effort may help them make more informed decisions.

I thank my many new friends and insiders who shared time and insights with me: Prentice-Hall for letting me use three interviews from my previous book, *Rebuilding Wall Street*; my skilled editor at Wiley, Myles Thompson; my agent, Anita Diamant; and Nicola Meaden, the energetic head founder of London-based Tass financial information agency. Additional helpful friends and acquaintances are Charles Epstein, Greg Bresiger, Jeff Sheran, Dan Delosa, Phil Maher—whom I forgot to thank in my last book—and especially Evan Simonoff.

A note on the interview process. Most interviews were conducted by telephone and recorded through extensive notes, then condensed into first-person narratives and, finally, fact-checked. A courtesy review was allowed.

I am a reporter, not an expert in financial matters. I have tried to write this book as simply as possible, with the help of my insiders, but I have not tried to define each and every financial term; readers can find definitions in financial dictionaries.

The financial insiders who gave so generously of their time and knowledge helped me understand the global financial industry. None of them is in any way responsible for the ultimate organization of this book or its conclusions. Any mistakes are my own. If I have included any source material without attribution, I apologize in advance.

MARK FADIMAN

# CONTENTS

# INTRODUCTION

♦

## WHAT IS MARKETSHOCK?

Markets have always inflated, deflated, and crashed. Now computers move funds faster than ever, and markets respond even more quickly. The world's *de facto* information standard collides with vested business interests and regulators. Modern marketshock is the result.

In its purest form, marketshock is a collision of regulation and technology that leads to a swift movement in a market followed by an equally sharp countermovement. We saw this in 1987 when so-called program traders helped drive the U.S. stock market down some 500 points, in 1992 when international traders helped crash the global currency markets and early in 1994 when Federal Reserve rate increases helped spark a worldwide bond collapse. This book is intended to help individual investors overcome marketshock by using macromarket asset allocation to smooth out the velocity and volatility of their portfolios. The interviews with more than 50 top market insiders will help

1

readers understand how the financial system operates at home and abroad and what they need to do to protect themselves. This introduction includes a definition of marketshock, an explanation of how marketshock has evolved in terms of technology, an outline of marketshock as it relates to the modern fiat-money state and, finally, a summary of upcoming chapters and insider interviews.

Some history, first. Earlier in the nation's—and the world's—economic life, when currency was linked to gold, money was somewhat more stable than it is now. Throughout the 19th century and into the early 20th, economists tell us that in this country prices fluctuated less than 20 percent and inflation was virtually nil. Unfortunately, governments don't easily accept the discipline of asset-based money and often seek to overthrow it by severing the linkages. This is what happened worldwide in the 20th century. The final step in the delinking of gold from currency was accomplished by Richard Nixon on August 15, 1971, when he formally abrogated the post-war gold convertibility agreement of Bretton Woods. Economists and top money pros have been warning about increasingly unstable currencies ever since.

So-called fiat money, based on nothing but the faith and credit of the issuing government, is an invitation to financial instability, and certainly the late 20th century has seen its share. When money fluctuates, speculators step in, aggravating the fluctuation, while others seek elaborate hedging methods to compensate for the increased velocity of the bad currency. Computers now exacerbate speculative efforts, though it is the argument of this book that judicious computerized strategies across markets—along with business-cycle allocation—can also help investors cope with inevitable fluctuations, at least for the time being.

Computers, combined with the new information networks that can speed enormous amounts of data around the world, will continue to create new forms of speculation that will further shake an already shaky fiat-money world. In the late 20th century there are no guarantees that an investor who needs to remove money from certain investments at a certain time will not be the victim of a marketshock that leaves those investments at a low ebb just when they need them most. As more money moves around the world more quickly, using ever more complex strategies, these kinds of occurrences—marketshocks—will probably become more, not less, prevalent.

A marketshock starts with a triggering event. The worldwide stock collapse of 1987 actually began when bankers around the world tightened rates, squeezing the global economy. Markets topped out in 1987, but the downward "correction" that followed was a thoroughly modern one, enhanced by computers and powerful, if simplistic, program-trading strategies. It is probably no coincidence that the largest, most liquid exchanges, American physical exchanges, using jury-rigged communications and computer order mechanisms, were among those that fell the fastest and hardest. Domestic physical exchanges, like the New York Stock Exchange (NYSE), with an artificially centralized order flow and highly regulated, micromanaged procedures, couldn't cope. Computers and modern trading strategies collided with 300 years' worth of increasingly outdated financial systems—and the market plummeted.

Marketshock is an observable phenomenon. The modern marketshock demands modern (computerized) information technology and old-fashioned regulation. Marketshock flourishes when financial industries are artificially segmented and money flows in predictable patterns. Very thinly traded markets as well as lively markets are subject to marketshock.

A marketshock needs a trigger. When it occurs, chances are that it is confined to a single instrument class: stocks, bonds, real estate, or some other centralized market. But marketshocks spread. A downturn in stocks can influence bond prices; currency re-evaluations can have myriad financial effects.

Marketshocks aren't only short-term phenomena. There are long-term, more gradual marketshocks as well, and a marketshock can move a market up sharply as well as down. The kind of marketshock that matters most to the individual investor is the kind that moves the market down in a short, sharp burst. And no such marketshock, old or new, would be complete without the participation of the small investor. This investor's ubiquitous presence at the end of every market upsurge or financial fad is a signal to professional investors to leave.

Investors who understand the mechanism of marketshock will be in a better position to protect themselves from at least some unpleasant money surprises than those who still haven't grasped the enormous changes that technology has wrought in the financial industry. Those who are struggling with these changes must understand them before they are truly equipped for modern investing.

## COMPUTERS AND REGULATIONS COLLIDE

The computer is a fundamentally radical device, as powerful as fire, and it is changing the face of finance—and therefore the way that companies and countries do business. Computers are already capable of processing huge amounts of information quickly and coming up with results that allow traders to adjust their positions instantly. Computers are also good at creating new financial instruments, a capacity that is perhaps less understood than their ability to generate trading speed, since complex financial instruments in general aren't well understood.

Computers have burst the artificial barriers set up by financial regulators. They have allowed major Wall Street intermediaries—the Street's largest firms—for the first time to see the order flow that moves through their shops. They allow big intermediaries, and domestic hedge funds that receive Wall Street's tips, to make quick investment decisions based on the flow of information. Regulations that have grown up over the last 300 years to stabilize the market work the opposite way in the information age.

Throughout much of the securities industry's history, beginning with the French stock exchange, money has been made through mediation—the extraction of a fee for buying or selling a financial instrument. But nowadays, with more and more individual and institutional investors trading for themselves and with commissions shrinking from competition, securities players are attempting to make the transition to a business in which they make money by trading for their own account—proprietary dealing. These players—the big banks and securities firms here and overseas—are commonly known as the sell side, since they sell securities and financial strategies to the so-called buy side—mutual funds, pension plans, and private investors, among others.

The computer has changed life for the buy side as well as the sell side. Because of computers, even the biggest buy-side funds are able to use more and more strategies to trade a dizzying number of instruments. Yet the buy side's use of computers to offer new products and services has not been matched by the sell side's use of computers to offer new ways of trading securities.

Computers therefore create instruments of marvelous complexity, but many of them are traded the way they always have been, through a small group of dealers and then to an even smaller group of market makers (whether these market makers use telephones, as the National Association of Securities Dealers' (NASD) screen- and phone-based NASDAQ trading system does, or a specialist-stock-auction system, as the NYSE does, matters little).

The computer has enhanced the instruments and strategies

offered to the public, but the industry itself, aided by regulators and politicians, has so far resisted the application of computers and electronic trading nets to placing orders—buying and selling securities. Were electronic nets to replace exchanges like the NYSE, then the industry might be disintermediated. That's a fancy term that means dealers on Wall Street and elsewhere would lose access to the precious order flow that creates commissions and trading opportunities.

Dealers are not alone in taking advantage of the system as it is. Any pro with a hot hand and a good amount of money under management can benefit from order-flow information in the possession of the Wall Street crowd. In 1987 it was hedge funds and private managers who traded ahead of the crash; in 1994, as I finish this book, there are reports that some mutual fund managers, flush with cash, are doing the same thing with the nation's bull-run market. But mutual funds are still highly regulated vehicles with limitations on their trading, and it's doubtful that the bulk of mid-1990s market manipulations could be set off by public-fund cash. More likely, institutional and private cash remain the most combustible combination. However, the rash of mutual fund manager front-running speaks to the intractable issue of the corrosive power of order flows. Large, centralized cash flows will always dangle market-rigging temptations in front of professional money managers, and as the mutual fund mania has grown, more professional traders have set up their own fund shops. However the answer is not increased regulation, but decreased. Not more restrictive trading rules, but less. Not additional channeling of order flow in one direction, but a diminution.

These antidotes cut to the heart of the debate about markets: whether a so-called centralized market, one in which order flow is concentrated in one physical or electronic arena, is preferable to a series of disparate markets that may or may not be linked.

Unfortunately, as electronic marketplaces spring up around the country and around the world, arguments about centralization will become more vociferous because markets will become more fragmented. Money-industry interest groups will continue to fight hard to retain their archaic privileges. Yet, progress will prevail, as it must. Such arguments will become fainter as electronic nets begin to coalesce on their own and new unregulated market makers enter the scene. The result will probably be a series of electronic nets through which orders to buy and sell various types of instruments swim freely, interacting according to manifold, complex, mathematical strategies.

Such a system is a far cry from the narrow buying and selling of specific instruments that takes place on the crowded floors of physical exchanges, where the actual face-to-face presence of traders is required. That these systems still exist may be more a testament to the clout of the securities industry than to the appropriateness of these age-old trading systems.

Arcane arguments over physical exchange trading, dealer trading versus specialist auctions; debates over "inside" bids, "two-dollar" brokers and "hard" and "soft" consolidated limit order books (CLOBs)—these confusing discussions have been rightly tuned out by a public that doesn't want to hear and the media which, on the whole, don't understand. But the issues involved in the buying and selling of securities go to the heart of capitalism. And because Wall Street, regulators, and politicians have resisted, and continue to resist true electronic trading—the buying and selling of securities by those who actually own the securities—a good deal of investors' choices today are a chimera. Richness of strategy on the buy side has not been matched with a similar richness of electronic (computerized) trading on the sell side. Electronic exchanges like Steve Wunsch's Arizona Stock Exchange take years to negotiate regulatory hurdles. The combination of a computerized and deregulated buy side and a still-rigid sell side funneling orders through physical stock exchanges is a recipe for continued marketshocks.

In the era of marketshock, regulatory rigidity reinforcing the status quo is dangerous to investors. But these investors may not understand how much of our current financial system is organized by regulations that have piled up over the last 50 years—and regulations aimed at banking that go back hundreds of years in this country.

The nation's financial industry is something of an artificial creation, a layer cake with $2 trillion worth of pension funds at the bottom, money managers in the middle, and a handful of Wall Street firms at the top, where the icing is. In 1993 alone, Wall Street passed a historic but little remarked barrier when its top 10 firms broke the trillion dollar mark for public issuance. A handful of perhaps 10 firms issued, incredibly, more than $1 trillion worth of new stock and bond securities, according to Wall Street-based *IDD* magazine; some $850 billion in fixed income and $150 billion in equity. This kind of clout is just one small example of how concentrated trading and issuance really is. This system has its roots in European mercantilism but emerged, full-blown, in the United States, in the 19th century and was encouraged throughout the mid- and late 20th century by government financial industry officials. Why would regulators encourage such distorting protectionism and centralization? A centralized system ensures easier control of powerful Wall Street bankers. Of course this assumes government regulators are up to the task of policing a $1 trillion industry. A big task indeed. And now that the computer has come along, the Wall Street firms at the top of the heap—or cake—can see the order flow of the clients who are forced, by design, to trade through them.

Our financial industry is a series of segmented industries—

insurance, banking, securities dealing—each of which, on the surface, does something different. But push beneath the surface and the similarities are stronger than the differences. The computer will eventually erase remaining differences. Competition that breaks down barriers between financial industry sectors—real competition—is the answer to the problems of our troubled financial industry.

In my previous book, *Rebuilding Wall Street*, I listed just a few of the more significant rules affecting the U.S.'s larger financial industry that came to mind: Glass-Steagall, which set up the split between commercial banks and Wall Street firms; the McFadden Rule, which still makes it hard for banks to expand beyond state lines; Rule 390, which mandates that Wall Street firms cross certain trades on the floor of a recognized physical stock exchange; the short-short rule, which says mutual funds can't get more than a small amount of their income from transactions that are less than 90 days in length without losing tax advantages; the Investment Act of 1940, which mandates, in part, that all sellers of mutual funds charge the same prices for the same products; and the Employee Retirement Income Security Act (ERISA), which codifies how pension plans provide for their employees and what they can and can't invest in.

Such regulations were designed to diminish leverage and dampen financial innovation. In fact, the artificial structure that has grown up in this country over the last 300 years is a continuing invitation to instability. In the 1980s, we saw a savings and loan (S&L) bust that cost the country some $300 billion to $500 billion, limited partnership losses in real estate that cost investors some $200 billion, a junk bond crash that cost consumers maybe another $100 billion, penny-stock fraud that according to government reports cost investors another $20 billion, and other kinds of underperforming or badly thought-out Wall Street products like closed-end country funds and bond funds and real-estate investment trusts (REITs) that took another $40 billion to $50 billion from investors' pockets.

## COMPUTERS AND POLITICIANS COLLIDE

Economic regulation colliding with computerized financial strategies may produce marketshock. But modern marketshocks are also, at least in part, the product of government efforts to prime the economic pump through taxes and central banking policies. In simplest terms, governments use regulatory levers to inflate and deflate the economy—attempting to control the business cycle. In this country, the central bank is the Federal Reserve. Because our presidents are elected every four years, our economic cycles tend to be between four and eight years long—a reason why booms and busts tend to occur in decade-like segments: the Roaring Twenties, the Go-Go Eighties. But if Fed manipulation is a sparkplug of economic instability, the financial euphorias that inevitably follow exaggerate it.

Of course, marketshocks in other guises have been around even before there were economists to track them and reporters to bemoan them. Harvard economist John Kenneth Galbraith, for instance, has traced the history of old-fashioned marketshocks— "speculative episodes," he calls them in his *Short History of Financial Euphoria*. Galbraith's argument is an updated version of Charles Mackay's *Extraordinary Popular Delusions and the Madness of Crowds*, the idea that speculation is inherent in markets and where speculation and leverage exist, a market mania will inevitably occur and eventually lead to a collapse.

Galbraith's arguments are both popular and seductive because financial systems are complex and it is difficult to say with any certainty exactly what factor caused which outcome. Galbraith even cites human nature's impulse to blame as a reason why explanations of financial booms and busts are offered—along with fingerpointing—with such vehemence after the fact.

However, while Galbraith may have a point about human nature, it seems clear that some economic models work better than others (the former Soviet Union is a good example) and that booms and busts—including market tops and tumbles—are not entirely due to chance. A growing group of neo-classical economists whose explanations make sense to me—the so-called Austrians—would maintain that financial euphorias are at least in part influenced by the larger business cycle and do not exist in isolation. They may be the products of "free" markets, but absent this freedom it is very difficult to tell whether a financial euphoria is simply a "madness" or whether the crowd has been driven into a frenzy by a market that has been artificially stimulated. Certainly the financial markets—stocks, bonds, and commodities—are immensely sensitive to government intervention through tax policy and Fed procedures. Unfortunately, as sensitive as financial markets are, computers make them more so. The computer is a tool as powerful as fire, but in this context it is also a magnifying glass, making euphorias move that much faster and making the fall that much harder.

It stands to reason that if computers make our financial markets more efficient and if they speed the movement of capital around the world, they can also reinforce dangerous financial trends. These trends, when set in motion by the government and reinforced by Wall Street's vast selling machine, are dangerous enough without computers' magnification. When government policies are subject to the enhancing effect of computerized finance, even small details are magnified. When free-market traders use screen-based trading technology to confront and undermine central banking initiatives, marketshock results—as it did in 1992 during the worldwide currency crash.

## MARKETSHOCK SOLUTIONS

This book is mostly about how individual investors can protect themselves in the era of marketshock. But since part of the problem is systemic—how the introduction of a new tool into a fiat-money environment turned the old order upside down— individual investors should be aware of some changes that can help not only their own plight but also the larger system.

*Systemic Solutions.* Sooner or later regulators will realize that the most successful securities regulation has to do with changing the way the system operates and is regulated. Regulation (if we must have regulation at all) in the era of marketshock should be aimed at encouraging large market players to establish sensible risk controls and fast-moving leverage settlement. Regulations that are respectful of free markets and human psychology are likely to be the least harmful approaches of the future. Regulations that encourage market pros to evolve such mechanisms are more useful—and less destructive—than those aimed at reinforcing an archaic status quo made up of physical-exchange systems and rigidly defined financial sectors.

Additionally, "electronic sunshine," the dissemination of prices and other information about financial markets, might help protect individual investors from the worst kind of market euphorias. Financial regulations in this country are based on the notion of equal access to market information, but Washington's regulators have been extraordinarily slow in using screen-based technology to speed the flow of financial information to the general public. It is no coincidence that some of the worst abuses of the 1980s—limited partnerships, junk bonds, and penny stocks— were all markets in which prices were known only to a few and could be easily manipulated. Basically, our financial industry—which includes banking and insurance—is a confused mish-mash of government regulations and "free" enterprise. Sometimes it seems like every conceivable risk to the consumer is to be rectified by government regulation, yet all this really does is further calcify an antedated system that was never built on sound economic principles.

The financial industry's rigid segmentation means increasing trouble for financial industry subsets outside of securities dealing and underwriting. In the 1980s, S&Ls, a peculiar and outdated banking industry subset of the financial industry, were sunk by a lethal cocktail of high rates, lax accounting standards, and government insurance.

In the 1990s, savvy insiders speculate that the powerful insurance industry, girded by similar archaic regs, could be the next to topple. These observers say that insurance, especially life insurance, is a product of a stable money environment that allowed this kind of business to match fixed-income instruments to life expectancy. The only trouble is that in an inflation-prone, fiat-money system, bonds tend not to hold their value. Additionally, state regs may mandate certain kinds of fixed-income investing. What's the result? Insurers, whipsawed by inflation, weighed down by regulation engendered by their own lobbying efforts, increasingly turn to the consumer to extract fees in lieu of investment profits—a solution bound to backfire with potentially explosive results. In the era of marketshock, no financial subset is immune.

Without analyzing each problem and each regulation separately, a task beyond the scope of this book, it is nonetheless easy to identify the problem at the heart of the matter: government has increasingly taken on the task of compensating individuals for financial industry disasters.

This has at least three effects. First, the money industry becomes beholden to government at local, state, and federal levels since the government is the payer of last resort. Second, segments of the financial industry, not having to worry about solvency, become careless—as we saw with the terrible losses registered by S&Ls. And third, government, concerned about its investment, continually constrains and reorganizes the financial industry. Unfortunately, many of the regs that government directs at the financial industry are developed with the help of the leading players in the industry and thus tend to reinforce the status quo rather than buttress safety and solvency.

The obvious solution would be to get government out of the business of insuring the financial industry. Various schemes have been suggested for government and private-industry financial partnerships, including so-called cross-guarantee insurance. But there is no reason why the market can't do the same job of insuring our various financial industries as effectively or more effectively than the public regulators. And government, lacking the pretext it has to "regulate" the financial industry to insure consumers' safety, would suffer a corresponding loss of power. Private insurance for our financial industries would have another positive effect in that because industry players would no doubt be paying for the privilege of being scrutinized by insurers, these players would think carefully about taking risks that might downgrade their creditworthiness. Additionally, private individuals, purchasing financial insurance against a certain level of losses—including losses due to fraud or criminality—would remember, whenever they wrote out a check to the private insurer, that modern, fiat-money investment is a risky game, one that demands considerable care and prudence.

*Individual Solutions.* It is true—as perceptive financial pundits and reporters like Walter Wriston, Paul Gibson, and Joel Kurtzman have all pointed out recently—that the new information (electronic money) standard combined with increasingly sophisti-cated software, misguided regulations, and financial-industry clout spells volatility with a capital V. More markets in the 21st century, linked to each other by a variety of information channels, will move more quickly than in the 20th. Additionally, new ways of investing through mutual funds—even new ways of organizing mutual funds through the so-called hub and spoke strategy, for example (whereby a fund may set up commingled asset pools anywhere in the world)—will allow investors more access to more markets than ever before.

Investors can surrender to the inevitable—savings that ebb and flow with disconcerting frequency—or become more savvy. I would suggest the investor consider something I have reluctantly ended up calling macromarket business-cycle asset allocation—business-cycle allocation for short. Let's break down these con-cepts. First of all, the investor ought to consider placing assets in each and every market available. Not the stock market or the bond market or the metals market or the real estate market, but every one of them. In the age of computerized investing marketshock can rapidly afflict one or several markets. Post-computer, a savvy investor talking about the market will mean the *macromarket*, the entire international universe of available assets. ˙

Investors who have read this book and subsequently done their own homework will soon realize how much of the nation's and the world's economy is subject to the decisions of central bankers and politicians. By understanding the fiat-money reflationary and deflationary triggers available to those in power, investors will be better able to discern for themselves where a particular region or asset class fits into the larger *business cycle*. Finally, an investor who uses *asset allocation* has placed money in a so-called diversified portfolio of securitized instruments, usually stocks and bonds.

Marketshock savvy investors will combine the above three

concepts when making investment decisions. They will investigate the broadest spectrum of markets, understand where in the business-cycle markets and instruments reside and allocate assets accordingly. In a disinflation, for instance, securitized instruments such as stocks and bonds are likely good investments. In a mildly reflationary environment, tangible assets such as real estate, metals, and certain stock sectors will become more profitable.

As with any judicious investment strategy, the investor must keep in mind that some level of macromarket diversification across most asset classes and regions is a necessity. However, investors who are confident of their choices and willing to make big bets may end up involved with what the securities industry calls market timing.

Market timing is a dirty word for some of those involved with the securities industry because timing strategies seem to imply that the individual investor can outwit the stock market, the market to which timing strategies are ordinarily applied. Many securities advisers and much of the financial media recommend that investors simply place their cash in stocks and wait. The reader of this book may not be so inclined. In fact, the boldest investors who apply business-cycle allocation to their portfolios may end up with extreme allocation weightings resembling market-timing strategies.

It does seem to me that aggressive asset-class investing and reweighting may be the investing of the future for a simple reason: Electronic trading is "commoditizing" more and more asset classes. What is a commoditized market? When instruments such as stocks are traded in blocks (often in groups called indexes) these stocks become more valuable in aggregate than individually. If an investor believes that the markets around the world are undergoing a fundamental change based on this commoditization, he or she will want to consider business-cycle allocation as a strategy for at least a portion of available funds.

Of the three concepts that form business-cycle allocation, the most difficult for the individual investor to internalize will probably be the business cycle itself. And the most difficult portion of business-cycle theory is probably the idea that governments around the world are the culprits behind the booms and busts that afflict modern-day capitalism.

The famous Austrian economist Ludwig von Mises was apparently the first to propound the theory that government monetary policy was responsible for the boom-bust cycle of Western-style economies. Von Mises and his disciple, Friedrich A. Hayek, held that without such government intervention, capitalism would be subject to so-called fluctuations caused by entrepreneurial activity, but that great inflations and depressions would be mitigated or even dissipated.

This view is, unfortunately, still controversial. And in the past it is certainly not one that has served as a fulcrum of economic thought. Economists and pseudo-economists have maintained that capitalism gave rise inevitably to booms and busts and that it was the job of the state to alleviate them. Karl Marx's ideas were perhaps the most radical response to the boom-bust view of capitalism while John Maynard Keynes's less extreme solutions gained credence, sadly, in the West throughout the mid- and late 20th century.

According to Austrian theory, most everything that governments do to allay recessions has the reverse effect, making matters worse: The Great Depression is only the most extreme example. Still, knowledge is power. Investors who understand how central banking policies and government wage and welfare policies stimulate and exacerbate the business cycle may be able to predict for themselves—in at least a general way—in which direction interest rates are headed and how severe a given recession may be.

This discussion may sound odd to investors used to hearing about the relative merits of load versus no-load funds and what annuities and retirement planning can do for their golden years. But this is not a how-to book for investors interested in the purchase of certain financial-industry instruments. What I am trying to do here is lift the veil and peer behind the instruments being peddled to take a look at the players themselves.

## THE ORGANIZATION OF THIS BOOK

This book presents insights from savvy insiders on how investors can protect themselves in the era of marketshock using business-cycle allocation across markets and regions. It begins by introducing and explaining the problem of marketshock. Below are summaries of chapters.

*Chapter One.* Insiders describe what marketshock is, how it is caused, and where it is headed. They explain the mechanisms of the financial industry and how computerization is fundamentally changing the way finance works here and abroad. These insiders also explain how the new technology interacts with regulatory authorities to cause marketshock.

In 1987, the stock market crash was exacerbated by program trading in which the buy side—pension plans and other small-investor pools of money—sought to hedge exposure through various rudimentary kinds of strategies using the stock and futures markets. What was forgotten in all of this was twofold. First, by using essentially the same strategies, the industry was ensuring that sooner or later the strategies would cease to be efficacious since not everyone can exit through the same door at once (as those who analyzed the debacle after the fact put it). Second, the dealers, those who were selling the insurance to the so-called buy side, knew the triggers for the strategies, the points at which the institutions would either buy or sell stocks or financial futures.

The situation is not so different now, though the names have changed. Big sell-side entities—Wall Street and certain sophisticated smaller dealers and banks—are now selling so-called derivatives to the buy side, the mutual funds and institutions that are lining up to purchase them.

In simplest terms, a derivative is a bet on which way certain financial instruments and interest rates are going to move at a given time. The process is the same as it was when institutions were buying so-called portfolio insurance from Wall Street. Just as was the case then, a large amount of order flow is being funneled through a small group of dealers who then swap the risk back and forth between themselves, having taken their profit up front. Surely such a scenario is ripe for marketshock.

*Chapter Two.* This section attempts to familiarize average investors with regional economic activity around the world. Insiders also analyze what makes an economy tick. The U.S. economy, with its high interest rates and low savings rates, is not the ideal investment climate for a savvy investor's money. This person may well want to seek out other, more promising regions for at least a small portion of investments.

What makes healthy economies tick are non-invasive, fair taxes, relatively low and steady interest rates and high savings rates. Modest rates guarantee that most private business can borrow based on the expectation of a steady return that will pay off borrowings. If business can borrow with a certainty of low rates, the economy will probably grow more steadily. A high savings rate is important because banks need money to lend to businesses and entrepreneurs. No savings, no lending. Efficient economies are predictable. Interest rates are not manipulated for political gain. Risk is not unduly penalized, nor are rewards.

Economists who favor private market solutions would caution that such an environment must at least to some degree arise spontaneously. The government cannot simply mandate low, steady interest rates (nor high savings rates) and expect an economic miracle and neither can an eager investor. However, it does seem apparent that certain authoritarian governments like Singapore and Taiwan have been at least partially successful in grafting free-market principles onto rigid and sometimes nasty regimes. Long-term, of course, the savvy investor will understand that the stability of such governments—and therefore the performance of the economy—is not insured. (The dismembering of Japan's monolithic, postwar social order proceeds apace even as I write.) But in the shorter term, over a period of years and even decades, the investor may find that his democratic sentiments, no matter how laudable, have a deleterious effect on his wallet.

*Chapter Three.* In this section, investors begin to learn how to get a portion of their savings abroad most efficiently. Investors can, of course, study other languages and spend time familiarizing themselves with the business and economic scenes of diverse foreign climes. Or they can invest in a private or public fund. For purposes of brevity I refer to most international money run by the larger (buy-side) fund companies as Big Money.

Big Money is invested in recognizable—and often simplistic—ways. The investing strategy that mainly flourished among individual investors as well as mutual funds before the computer is known as value investing. Value investing has to do with finding a stock or some other instrument or property that is supposedly undervalued in comparison to a larger market of similar items. Value investors tend to buy and hold; that is, having identified a valuable if underpriced investment, an investor who is pursuing a value-investment strategy would keep the purchase for a lengthy period of time to maximize gain. This kind of investment strategy sounds simple, but there is a trick, and a hard one at that: identifying the valuable, underpriced instrument in the first place.

Another kind of precomputer investing is known as technical investing. In the past, this was mainly a haven for money pros who loved to pore over charts seeking patterns in markets, mainly the stock market, that could be recognized ahead of time. Rudimentary technical investing strategies might be said to include strategies developed by hedge funds in which the money pro attempted to hedge by simultaneously buying and selling the same, or similar, stocks.

Like any other investment strategy, technical investment probably works best as a tool employed along with other tools. Recently, with the spread of the personal computer, cost-effective tools have emerged that allow professional investors to use a wider gamut of information and mathematical analysis to invest in a broad array of securities.

Today, professional investors who use computers intensively for investment purposes are often called quants—short for "quantitative," the methodology such investors are said to have adopted. Financial writer Peter Bernstein in his great book, *Capital Ideas* (The Free Press, 1992), traced the evolution of quantitative investing which has kept pace, not surprisingly, with the development of the computer. Many investment pros who could be characterized as quants subscribe to the idea—one that has gained credence in the last 50 years—that it is difficult to beat the market by picking individual securitized instruments.

Of course, while quantitative investing often does give institutions and increasingly individuals disciplined diversification within a universe of securitized instruments, such investing has far to go to realize its potential. This is because quantitative investing has its roots in the stock industry, and therefore the broader diversification across tangible asset classes, real estate, metals, etc., is almost always lacking in the offerings of quant money managers.

At its most basic, quantitative investing seeks to analyze investors' risk tolerance to produce a so-called efficient frontier. Instruments are then selected that will produce the maximum gain without generating more risk than is allowable. Often instruments used by a quant are selected in aggregate. Such aggregate instruments are called "indexes." As quantitative investing has evolved, indexes have been sliced and diced into subindexes that can be weighted in various ways. By customizing a "plain vanilla" index, the quant is hoping to generate a more generous return while minimizing risk.

Quantitative investing has changed the face of finance. Even Big Money mutual funds are not immune and are employing more and more quantitative strategies, just as hedge funds and Wall Street firms are. Surprisingly, domestic regulators have let these international strategies flourish for the time being. The Securities and Exchange Commission (SEC) has been letting new mutual funds trade in a variety of markets (though as this manuscript was going to press, Congress was announcing a drive to scrutinize, overhaul, and tighten fund regulations). There are funds—as well as private money managers—that now trade only international equity futures, that switch back and forth between currencies, options, and metals, and that hedge using sophisticated interbank techniques to protect their gains.

I call some of these funds—both large and small—New Money, to distinguish the techniques that are being used and the results being gained from the Big Money funds (and private money managers) of the past that have mainly concentrated on one sector over a long time period. This is the subject of Chapter Four.

*Chapter Four.* The reason that New Money funds have come into existence is that the old-fashioned methods of buying for the long term are less effective in the era of marketshocks and computer technology, when whole investment segments are breaking down and blending.

New Money comes in a variety of flavors. In addition to funds that can sell short and buy a broad variety of asset classes, New Money can be defined by industry type. In this country so-called hedge funds are an exploding segment of international New Money. These funds cater primarily to moneyed investors, but their services will be increasingly affordable as competition pushes down fees. Hedge funds are free to invest in whatever they choose, though traditionally they have bought long and sold short in the stock market to provide both safety and profit to individual investors. Hedge funds are investing in a lot more than stock now. In fact, "hedge fund" is starting to be a misnomer because these funds are beginning to take huge, unhedged international bets. Hedge funds may invest in futures, in options, in real estate. The legendary hedge fund master, George Soros, invests in all of these and more.

A defining factor of New Money is its use of computers and computerized investment strategies. International hedge funds are the beneficiaries of computerized investing—even when they don't make extensive use of computers themselves—because of the digitalized information flows and new kinds of products that computers are creating. New Money funds using artificial intelligence techniques to invest with are obvious beneficiaries of computers and computing power. Public and private Big Money funds that increasingly use quantitative technologies also benefit.

As quantitative investing evolves, money pros increasingly move in and out of various indexes and subindexes in various asset classes according to certain economic and market-based signals. Market timing is a controversial strategy, but quantitative investment styles lend themselves to it, and this form of investing as well as aggressive asset allocation will increase, not decrease, as more computer power is applied to investing around the world.

The New Money trend is accompanied by another trend that has been referred to as Hot Money, the focus of Chapter Five.

*Chapter Five.* Hot Money invests in the exploding worldwide futures arena. Hot Money is leveraged money because the way the futures markets are set up allows for significant leverage. Of course, there is no reason that other markets should not also offer additional leverage, and indeed in this country stock market investing used to offer more leverage until the 1929 Crash and subsequent takeover of leverage authority by regulators.

There are dangers in offering untrammeled leverage to a broad group of consumers, but it is also possible that the danger of leverage is, at least to a degree, related to time, not size. Leverage-heavy Chicago futures markets require traders to pay off losses at the end of every day. Losses are sustained but controlled.

Like New Money, Hot Money is a beneficiary of the computer, since the futures market has encouraged investment styles that are sympathetic to technology's evolution. Futures markets trade contracts—portions of single instruments—and these contracts have remarkable similarities to equity-index instruments traded by quants. Futures instruments are therefore tailor-made for computerized investing; you could say that futures players' fast, hedged, computerized trading is, at least in part, the future of securities trading.

Imagine physical-exchange systems reduced to elements of screen trading. The institutional or individual investor must internalize the concept that there are no "futures" markets, no "stock" markets—not even separate financial industries—in retail banking, investment banking, insurance, or securities sales. Rather, all kinds of financial transactions are merely points on a yield curve that can be reduced to electronic blips on a screen.

The marriage of the computer and Wall Street is not necessarily positive for individual investors. Our system, with its artificially concentrated, centralized order flow—mimicked by the rest of the world—allows Wall Street firms as well as international investment banks the kind of terrible clout that has exaggerated financial fads in the past. The forces that regulators are playing with now are more powerful on an order of magnitude than those that have ever been experienced before. As computers throw more and more money into the system, as neural nets increase the velocity with which money travels around the world, investors are going to need all the help they can get. Chapter Six provides this help.

*Chapter Six.* In this final section, top professional advisers give their thoughts on what's next for the domestic and international financial scene. Such advisers may help small investors understand nuances of the business cycle and also help them position their accounts accordingly. The downside to such a strategy is that these professionals are often brokers or financial consultants who work for Wall Street firms and therefore may have an interest in selling the customer products that do more for the firm's purse than the client's. Accordingly, a small investor might seek out several different financial consultants to ensure that the advice is appropriate to the economic conditions and to the investor's ultimate goal of international diversification.

This is not to say that the investor is incapable of understanding economic trends. Through the act of investing, consulting with financial advisers and studying the subject, the small investor may soon begin to make more informed decisions and invest more independently and wisely.

In truth, business cycles—and thus investment cycles—are not especially complex, though certainly they are not simple either. For instance, as I finish this book, a number of economic scenarios could soon play themselves out. We may see a continued, gradual upturn in the economy, along with continued gentle growth in stock and bond markets. However, war, especially in the Middle East, acts of God, or renewed totalitarianism in the former Soviet Union, could change an economic scenario overnight.

In monetary terms, change is contained. Given current government policies, there are only two choices, actually: reflation and deflation (or their subsets, inflation and disinflation). In the case of real-money deflation, cash is certainly king. First of all, paper money, the dollar, becomes the repository of increasing value. Then perhaps foreign currencies, or even precious metals, as confidence erodes. Real estate, securities, and other asset-based investments become devalued in a deflation.

In a reflation, things are perhaps easier to predict, at least on a macrolevel. Tangible assets are a store of increasing value; commodities, real estate, and inflation-resistant securities are all good choices. Investors, however, must pay their money and take their chances. Those who do not want to choose will diversify broadly beyond stocks and bonds, keeping some assets in gold or money markets, as well as in low-fee principal-guaranteed managed futures funds if investors can find good ones. They will hope that whatever happens does not so overwhelm any one sector of the market as to render a swath of their portfolio worthless. In the very long term, we will ultimately see reflation, since rates are low as I write. The trick for canny investors will be to recognize reflation before it happens and make wise investment choices to realign portfolios—and possibly to sit out the attendant marketshocks.

I have chosen to use the word "reflation" rather than "inflation" because the former implies a conscious activity behind money movements. If there is one thing that I have learned in my conversations with financial insiders, it is that market trends are not random occurrences. Taxes, regulations, Federal Reserve policy, these are the levers that the powerful lean on, on behalf of the "public good." But too rarely, it seems, the public good is compatible with the leaner's own narrow agenda.

The next decades may well see an upswell in totalitarian or fundamentalist regimes; it may see immensely destructive warfare. But I think that for Western democracies, the real field of battle will be waged by those who want to use increasingly powerful information technologies to go against the status quo. Investors who understand the realities of the system will be better prepared to face the future on a variety of personal and financial levels.

Former president of Crédit Suisse's U.S. asset management group, Kenneth Tarr, says that in every generation there takes place one catastrophic market event in which most people lose most of their money. The best prepared of this generation will lose the least.

## CHAPTER ONE

# MARKETSHOCK

◆

## Technology, Regulation, and International Investing

This chapter presents views of money pros on how technology and regulation are colliding and how investors can protect themselves. First, insiders examine the technology of investing: where it's been, how it's changed, and where it's going. Next, they look at domestic securities regulation as well as domestic and international central banking. The idea is to tease out the various sources of conflict and isolate how regulatory initiatives can complement as well as collide with technology. Finally, they introduce international investing and strategies that individual investors can use—diversification and macro asset allocation—to try to protect themselves in the era of marketshock.

*Technology.* In order to understand the opportunity—as well as the risks—and be in the best position to take advantage of what is occurring, investors must first understand the true nature of modern investing. What is occurring is an unprecedented undermining of business as usual by technological innovation. The computer is an instrument of fundamental change, and more and more the change that it has introduced is taking effect and redefining power and money.

The computer has already changed finance domestically and abroad. Money can now move anywhere in an instant and in a nearly infinite variety of guises. The entire infrastructure of finance—the banks, securities firms, and physical exchanges that have held sway so long, huddling together on the tip of Manhattan, in Chicago's Canyon, in London's City—are essentially relics of a past era, monuments to a different economic environment.

Let's move beyond the physical evidence to the more substantive and important changes taking place. These changes go hand-in-hand with the computer and began in the 1960s as the impact of the computer began to be felt. Perhaps the first sign of what was to come was the cash management account, introduced by Merrill Lynch, which mimicked checking accounts and signaled the beginning of a war between two of this country's most rigidly regulated sectors, banking and stock dealing. That wasn't all by any means. Computers let the Chicago exchanges create financial futures, indexed instruments that bet on the movement of stocks and bonds. Essentially Chicago futures traders had discovered how to play the stock market without being there.

Once financial futures were created, it was only a matter of time before the suggestion surfaced that someone could make a bet on both futures and stocks. This bet was called portfolio insurance, and it was at least in part responsible for the violence of the crash of 1987, when the stock market fell in this country some 500 points in a day.

Today Wall Street firms are selling derivatives—essentially another bet (or hedge) on markets—to the same funds and institutions that bought portfolio insurance. Technology makes derivatives possible since the complex calculations that take place aren't available without computers. But a similar marketshock may result if too many institutions buy too many of the same kinds of derivatives at home and abroad, or if Wall Street's inter-dealer risk-swapping gets out of hand.

There is a problem with the way the computer has affected the financial industry: It is creating a dangerous imbalance of application. In the United States, there are more than 4,000 mutual funds, for instance, plus at least 7,000 active private money managers and hundreds of hedge funds. But the vast majority continue to trade through a handful of Wall Street firms that control the actual buying and selling function. This is called "centralization" by securities industry executives who claim that without a "central market," trading would break down. In fact, in the era of computerization, electronic markets, which allow buyers and sellers to interact with each other without Wall Street brokers in between, are the necessary element of a securities market, not centralization in the old-fashioned sense.

Computers allow professional investors to create thousands of new financial products, but the order flow generated by these products is still controlled and manipulated by only a relatively few industry players. Additionally, much public and private buy-side money, despite the evolving richness of strategy, is run under time-honored supervisory strategies employed by securities regulators. It can take two years or even longer to set up a public fund (so there are many more funds than companies running them), and mutual fund prices, ironically enough, still remain fixed, leading to confusing price levels, each one apparently subject to regulatory scrutiny. The combination of intricate products and rigid regulatory control and exchange mechanisms creates a marketshock waiting to happen.

*Financial Regulation.* Bureaucracies have always resisted change, so it's no surprise that regulators continue to come up with ways to "rationalize" markets and create so-called level playing fields. In Washington over the last five years, partly in reaction to the crash of 1987, there has been a regulatory overhaul of the financial industry that House Telecommunications and Finance Subcommittee head Edward Markey has called the most far reaching since the securities acts of the 1930s that created the Securities and Exchange Commission (SEC), the National Association of Securities Dealers (NASD), and most of the attributes of the regulatory regime that has been in force for the last 50 years.

Recently the SEC and other regulators, mostly through acts of Congress, have been granted new, widespread powers. The SEC, for instance, now has authority to look at trading data to see if manipulation is taking place and also to look at the books of securities firms to ensure they are solvent. In the case of the futures markets, the Federal Reserve has been given the right to set some margins to ensure that speculation doesn't get out of control. Some of this regulation is vaguely systemic in nature; the government is giving the SEC the right to look at firms' subsidiary books to see if the firms are solvent. But leaving aside the economic arguments, the idea of the SEC examining large trades in an effort to determine whether a manipulation has occurred is increasingly ridiculous. For one thing, manipulation includes the establishment of intent, so unless it can be proven there was a conspiracy to defraud, the traders may well get away unscathed by maintaining that they just didn't know. For another, technology is rapidly approaching the point at which it will be difficult to tell what an artificially intelligent program has traded versus what a trader has made a decision to do. Eventually the SEC may find itself in the position of banning the use of certain kinds of software, a position that would be hard to maintain in any society that gives lip service to free markets.

Human nature being what it is, the result of regulatory collision with free markets will lead to ever-greater opportunities abroad but only for those who understand the fundamentals of what is occurring and are able to act on that knowledge.

*Central Banking.* Once an investor has internalized marketshock, he or she must take the next step—determining what to do. This book suggests diversification across asset classes and strategies at home and abroad using commonsense business cycle knowledge to determine the best placement for at least some assets at a given time.

In order to understand how business cycles work, it is helpful to examine the one economic theory that seems to explain modern economic fluctuations, the Austrian business-cycle theory. In simplest terms, this theory, originally developed by Austrian economists Ludwig von Mises and Friedrich Hayek, blames capitalist booms and busts on government profligacy. The stage is set once government has passed laws that allow it to control and print money. Soon it's in a position to inflate to cover spending beyond what tax revenues allow. In our country government does this in part by borrowing money and also by selling notes and bonds to itself and then allowing private banks to lend against these expanded, fictitious reserves—an act that eventually fuels inflation. Once inflation begins, consumers spend more and raw material producers, getting the message, raise prices. Unfortunately, the boom is temporary because government will ask its central bankers to raise private market bank rates to slow down the economy's so-called growth. A recession begins, one that lasts until government again applies the artificial stimulus of borrowed money, thus kick-starting inflation. The danger of course is hyperinflation or massive deflation, and the 20th century has seen some of each.

Austrian economists hold that, to restrain the government spending that leads to boom-bust cycles, governments must relink currency to an underlying asset, preferably gold. A currency linked to a specific underlying commodity is not an easily inflatable currency, though its true that throughout history government has managed to debase even gold-linked currency if it remains the primary controller of the money supply.

Barring some worldwide catastrophe, it seems unlikely that our current international monetary system will be brought back onto a gold standard anytime soon. If fiat money is to be valued against some underlying asset in the future, it may be something that future citizens regard as more valuable than gold, especially if technology eventually makes the production of gold easy and cheap. One possibility is that money may be relinked to a knowledge base such as software, since in the future software may be the most valuable commodity of all. Of course, investors may not find such speculation entertaining. The fiat-money environment they confront is all too real, and all too dangerous.

*International Investing.* Investors who want to protect themselves against marketshocks linked to fiat-money reflations and disinflations should pay careful attention to the effects that Fed rate manipulations may have on their investments. Internationally, disinflation will continue in some sectors of the globe until the mid-1990s, but in the United States, rates probably won't go much lower than as of this writing in early 1994. It's only a question of when they'll go back up. If they go up soon and fast, the effect on the marketplace will be harsh: Swollen stock funds will lose cash, and the stock market will move down quickly. Investors who have given in to yield's temptation will find themselves on the wrong side of a nasty leveraged downturn in bonds.

In this country and abroad, the easiest steps that can be taken to ameliorate marketshock are twofold. First, responsible regulators and financiers should encourage the release of as much information as possible about financial instruments. They should also try to break down physical-exchange mechanisms and the barriers between trading of various instruments. Second, lacking regulatory action, savvy investors should diversify their portfolios across regions, strategies, and asset classes. They should take the time to understand the business cycle and act on that information to readjust their portfolios when necessary.

# TECHNOLOGY

◆

## Overview

### *"Technology tends to undermine regulation."*

JEFF LAUTERBACH *is a senior vice president at the national independent securities firm, Financial Service Corp. A savvy securities watcher, Lauterbach predicted many of the industry's current trends in a 1987 book he cowrote,* The Revolution in Financial Services.

Technology is the lever that moves business. One example is Merrill Lynch's going into the banking business through its cash management account, a money-market account with check-writing privileges. Merrill Lynch kept track of customers through what was for the time a sophisticated computer system. This cash management account was one of the first real breaches in the post-1920s regulatory setup in this country.

Technology tends to undermine regulation. For the most part in this century, regulation has failed as a policing tool. Instead, people have used it as a competitive tool, seeking to get regulations written that give them an advantage over competitors.

As technology breaks down barriers, the financial industry in this country and abroad will become more competitive. I also think there will be more high-quality manufacturers of financial product and more high-quality distributors who are driven by consumer need.

◆

## Information Standard

### *"This enormous flow of data has created a new world monetary standard."*

WALTER WRISTON *is the famous former chairman of Citicorp; the following excerpt is from his book,* The Twilight of Sovereignty *(Charles Scribner's Sons).*

The information revolution is usually conceived, quite rightly, as the set of changes brought on by "information technologies," the two most important being modern communications technologies for transmitting information and modern computer systems for processing it. The marriage of these two technologies is now consummated. It is impossible to tell where communications stops and where computing begins. After years of study, in an attempt to determine which bureaucracy should have regulatory power, the federal government gave up on efforts to draw this distinction. In addition to powerful effects on culture and the pace of life, this revolution has changed what we do for a living. It has made many or most of us into what Peter Drucker long ago called "knowledge workers."

The marriage of the computer with telecommunications, resulting in a movement of information at the speed of light and to enormous audiences, tends to decentralize power as it decentralizes knowledge. When a system of national currencies run by central banks is transformed into a global electronic marketplace driven by private currency traders, power changes hands. When a system of national economies linked by government-regulated trade is replaced—at least in part—by an increasingly integrated global economy beyond the reach of much national regulation, power changes hands.

This enormous flow of data has created a new world monetary standard, an Information Standard, which has replaced the gold standard and the Bretton Woods agreements. The electronic global market has produced what amounts to a giant vote-counting machine that conducts a running tally on what the world thinks of a government's diplomatic, fiscal and monetary policies.

That opinion is immediately reflected in the value the market places on a country's currency.

Governments do not welcome this Information Standard any more than absolute monarchs embraced universal suffrage. Politicians who wish to evade responsibility for imprudent fiscal and monetary policies correctly perceived that the Information Standard will punish them. The size and speed of the worldwide financial market doom all types of central bank intervention, over time, to expensive failure. Moreover, in contrast to former international monetary systems, there is no way for a nation to resign from the Information Standard. No matter what political leaders do or say, the screens will continue to light up, traders will trade and currency values will continue to be set not by sovereign governments but by global plebiscite.

JOEL KURTZMAN *is editor of the prestigious* Harvard Business Review *and a former* New York Times *columnist. As author of the perceptive book,* The Death of Money, *Kurtzman staked a claim as a leading New Money observer.*

If we're on any standard at all, it's the information standard, but I'm not sure how stable a standard that is. Economies need stability to produce goods, but it's more profitable right now to speculate than to invest in plants. That's not the way economies should work.

If you had a stable currency system, you could deregulate, and I would certainly like to see it. If we had that anchor in the currency, we wouldn't worry so much about speculation and trading games. We wouldn't have to regulate so much because the slack would be taken out of the system. If money were linked to some form of commodity, where buying power would be preserved, the system would immediately lose its volatility.

Some country is going to have to take a lead and set up a

stable system, a link to the real world. Right now I couldn't say which that would be. There have been considerable marketshocks in Europe because of currency crises. Linking currency to a basket of consumer goods might be a reasonable way to go. If you said that the purchasing power of a hundred dollars is equal to a certain market basket of perhaps a dozen products together, traders could then work out what other currencies would be worth to buy the same basket, and we would begin to have stable currencies again. Then it would make sense to place savings in the bank since inflation is mostly the product of a fiat economy, and it would make sense to put cash in a place where it earned 3 percent.

Politicians often want to raise taxes on the wealthy because that's where the money is. But higher taxes are a disincentive to work, and one way or another, we're going to face the hard rock of reality.

◆

## THE 1987 CRASH

*"Everything can come tumbling down."*

GREGG KIPNIS *was a top trading executive at Morgan Stanley during the 1980s and later headed London-based NatWest bank's effort to build an international derivatives effort. Today he is head of the analytical trading division of Jefferies & Co.*

During the 1987 stock market crash, the exchange didn't know how to stop the traffic. They had no idea of the implications of the new strategies and technology fostered in the 1980s, like the Superdot system, which speeded trades electronically to the floor of the stock exchange. On top of that, the government made careless announcements on taxes. After one announcement, I knew exactly which 60 to 80 stocks would deflate—the takeover targets—and, if I knew them, others did too. It was a foolish statement—that Congress was thinking of making it punitive for anyone to do a leveraged takeover—and certain stocks, all the takeover stocks, just imploded. With that one statement, the government brought down the whole index. When panic comes at the wrong moment, there's a crash.

Internationally, markets are getting more complex and interrelated, not less so. All of the synthetic products created for investors that have the credit backing of the issuer are creating considerable secondary trading every day. Even in back-to-back trades, there's a ripple effect because somewhere down the line, someone else has to rehedge in the underlying market to accommodate what has been done. If there's ever a panic, it won't stop with people getting out of derivatives—it will also cause a concentration of trading in the underlying markets. I once hazarded a guess that as much as two-thirds of all the trading taking place is driven by some kind of derivative transactions.

There's a tremendous concentration of order flow through a few global firms—Morgan Stanley, Salomon Brothers, Merrill Lynch—and some big international players, the big Swiss banks, some of the largest Japanese firms like Nomura. The financial and economic regimes of all the different major countries are not integrated or harmonized. One currency and one economic policy might ease the situation, but maybe that's instituting a kind of market socialism. It would look benign but be highly rigid.

I remember the first time I read about plate tectonics and this new theory of earthquakes in *National Geographic* magazine. The author made some comment that I generalized to world affairs. As long as the plates of our varying worldwide economic structures and policies can slide by each other relatively smoothly, there will be no earthquake. But when they become interlocked and the pressures build, you are set up for a big jolt, a large explosion where everything can come tumbling down. Millions of investors would suffer and billions would be lost. It's vital that the world financial markets make dramatic changes to accommodate the ability of money and prices to move smoothly and to reflect the magnitude of wealth that has to move.

———————◆———————

## PORTFOLIO INSURANCE

### *"Everybody knew what the overhangs were."*

**BOB KIRBY,** *former chief investment officer of the $20 billion Capital Guardian Trust, was one of the members of the famous Brady Commission set up to investigate the 1987 stock market crash.*

The 1987 crash was kicked off by program trading and portfolio insurance. What happened was that everybody knew what the overhangs were—where the big institutions would have to sell because of their portfolio insurance strategies. Everybody knew the mathematics, so everybody knew what was coming, and that put more pressure on the market—except for players smart enough to be on the other side. Wall Street was on the other side, and so were some of the hedge funds. There were no clear-cut sides. It's never as clear as the media like to portray it. Chicago, New York, everybody is mixed up in it. It's an internecine kind of war, the way these things always are, but for public consumption, the NYSE pointed fingers at Chicago.

Of course, it confused the public. You don't want to be blamed for something like the crash. The White House had to get involved before the Depository Trust Company would disgorge the names of the players involved with the largest orders during the crash. When you found out they were some of the most responsible institutions in our country, it made you want to go lie down for a moment.

———————◆———————

## ELECTRONIC EQUITY

### *"Regulators tend to defend what's already in place."*

CARY GRANT *knows the securities industry from the inside out. A former Midwest Stock Exchange specialist and market maker, he is also the founder of a high-tech trading firm.*

The new kind of exchange is going to be totally electronic. Some exchanges are electronic already, like the currency markets and, to some extent the futures and fixed-income markets. Even stock markets are starting to move toward electronic trading, and unless the NYSE goes electronic, it won't be here.

Wall Street is more and more just a state of mind. Fidelity used to be thought of as a mutual fund, but it operates as a broker too, now, and not just as a broker but as an electronic broker. It has a system whereby orders come in and meet each other in a computer and match up. If they don't match up, Fidelity may try to match the orders anyway for its own account, or it can send the orders on to other electronic networks it's hooked up with. That's what's happening now: Electronic networks are linking up all over the country and all over the world.

There is another firm I know of that doesn't even need traders. The system trades itself and also lays off the risk through options. These systems are efficient and new, and they work well without specialists and floor brokers. The more systems that are developed, the more liquidity will be generated and the more efficient the market will be.

Regulators tend to defend what's already in place, but they should try to bring themselves up to speed on this subject. There are rules like NYSE Rule 390, which concentrates order flow on the floor of the NYSE. If those rules were removed, the NYSE would collapse. The big Wall Street firms would begin to internalize order flow—they would buy and sell customers' securities themselves, out of their own inventory, instead of looking for other buyers and sellers. These firms would essentially become market makers, specialists, but with much deeper pockets than most specialists have now.

There are worries about so-called internalization because the idea is that firms that are market makers could manipulate prices, but they do that anyway.

Here is what's going to happen: Small orders are going to be internalized, and large orders, institutional orders, are going to flow through worldwide global nets. Eventually both types of orders will meet and greet because they'll start to bundle order flow to give institutions more liquidity. They'll all be connected.

———————— ◆ ————————

## EXCHANGE DERIVATIVES

### *"Computers are powerful enough to work out margining requirements."*

NATE MOST *is a former head of new products for the American Stock Exchange. Under his watchful eye, the AMEX has produced a string of new products, including flexible, exchange-based derivatives.*

The big change in direction was our S&P Depository Receipts (SPDRs). We thought the SPDR product was a good idea because it let retail investors buy a single stock unit that was actually equivalent to the S&P index. Since most money managers underperform the index, we thought there would be considerable interest in a product that would allow retail investors to buy the index as some funds and institutions do. We've been very pleased with the result and are now trying to take SPDR-type products abroad.

We've set up an index that tracks the progress of the Tokyo stock exchange, and we'd like to offer a version of SPDRs for that as well. We'd like to give investors a number of international stock-unit alternatives.

It does tend to take time. It took a long time for SPDRs in part because this product was a new area. We were coming to the people at the SEC with a new concept. When you come with a new concept, things slow down. We were dealing with the regulatory group that oversees the 1940 act, and it took a while because the act was never intended to deal with this kind of product. After a fair amount of time and satisfying them that there was adequate protection, we now have about $500 million in the trust at this time, and we're trading 500,000 units or SPDRs a day.

We're also trading flex options, which offer customers the opportunity to customize certain option parameters. If you go to certain Wall Street firms and say you want to write a customized option, you can trade over-the-counter (OTC) and get any kind of option customization you want. We're an exchange, so we can't customize any option, but we will allow customization on certain instruments, such as our Japanese stock index, our major market index, and our institutional index.

The main reason we can offer these kinds of instruments now is that computers are powerful enough to work out margining requirements on these options-related derivatives. It used to be that you could offer only standardized options because that's all you'd figured out the margining for. Exchanges can't take the risk all by themselves. The seller of the option has to put up margin, and the Options Clearing Corp. has to say what that is. It has to take into account volatility, interest rates, and length of time for which the option is written. An exchange has to be able to determine all that quickly if it wants to offer customized options. Now we can.

Securities exchanges like ours offer customers advantages, including specialists, to guarantee liquidity in little-traded stocks and clearing that guarantees the creditworthiness of the trades that have been crossed on our floor.

———————◆———————

## DERIVATIVES OVERVIEW

### *"Derivatives, if properly used, can lessen risk, not increase it."*

DOUGLAS LUCAS *held one of the financial industry's most critical jobs as Moody's derivatives expert. He is now chief credit officer for Connecticut-based TMG, a subsidiary of Mutual Life of Canada.*

When we evaluate the credit quality of a commercial bank or a securities firm, we have to look not only at the balance-sheet risk but at the off-balance-sheet risk.

There are a number of questions we ask about the institution and also ask the institution. These questions fall into four general categories. First, we want an overview of what the firm's derivatives activity is. Then we want to know about market risk in the portfolio and how the bank or firm addresses the control of that risk. Third, we talk about the credit risk inherent in that portfolio, not only in terms of today's market value but in terms of potential future fluctuations. Finally, we talk about the operating risk—and that includes accounting and compliance and controls, as well as the expertise of staff involved in the derivatives business.

With a derivatives product, there are two characteristics to look at. First, let's define what a derivative is. It's a financial instrument whose price depends on another more fundamental, underlying instrument. By itself, a derivative has no inherent value. It has value only in relationship to the underlying instrument. There are different types of underlying instruments. There are different types of underlyings and different types of derivatives. The common underlyings are interest rates, currency rates, commodities, and equities.

The derivatives instrument itself could be an option, a forward, or a swap. We can build various combinations from the above lists, but at the most basic level, we're selecting one option from column A and one option from column B. That's how to build a derivative. The two things making up a derivative are the form of the commitment—whether it's an option or forward—and the underlying instrument—an interest rate or equity, for instance.

Depending on the type of derivative, the investor will trade either through an exchange or off-exchange—OTC. Exchange-traded derivatives are standardized. A common exchange-traded derivative would be an option on equity, something many investors have experience with. However, if an investor wanted an option out for more than a year, chances are he would have to find someone and do it away from the exchange. Private investors may have experience with options, but most have never been involved in currency and interest-rate swaps, where some of the largest derivatives volume is.

Dealers like the Wall Street firms—Salomon Brothers, Morgan Stanley, and J.P. Morgan—along with some large commercial banks will act as counterparties for customers like corporate clients who want OTC derivatives. If the dealer has acted as a market maker, making the trade itself, the dealer may elect to pass the risk of the transaction to another party by hedging with another dealer later in the day. Dealers make money on the order flow of their customers, and sometimes they'll choose to take a position, use their knowledge of customer order flow to see where demand is going, and try to get there first.

There are derivatives starting to come into use based on natural disasters. For example, you can buy an index of insurance losses— one is published by an independent insurance industry group— and use it to hedge risk as an insurer.

Derivatives are tools. They can lock in prices so that you're not surprised by some event you didn't count on. Derivatives, if properly used, can lessen risk, not increase it.

**I.W. "TUBBY" BURNHAM,** *one of the founders of Drexel Burnham Lambert, warned of the impending crash of 1987 in a now-famous memorandum to Drexel brokers.*

Something is going on with these derivatives that reminds me of the 1987 market crash and portfolio insurance. In 1987, funds were sold a strategy that was supposed to even out their risk. Instead, they found that when they tried to operate the strategy, they couldn't all do it at once. The market went down so quickly that the mechanisms that the funds counted on to work didn't.

The same thing is happening with derivative securities. Derivatives are a bet on the market. The parties try to hedge their risk, which is what portfolio insurance was all about. But the same Wall Street players that sold portfolio insurance are selling derivatives. And they're taking their fees on the front end even for five-year hedges. Nobody can buy a five-year hedge, so eventually the players will have to rehedge—sell the risk to someone else. This is fine until the market starts to move down fast. In a choppy, fast-moving market, it's hard to rehedge, and then it's not going to work any better than portfolio insurance did. These are rolling hedges that are being sold.

The trouble is the same as it's always been. Wall Street firms sell these products to the funds that think the products are going to work the way the firms say they will. But they don't.

---◆---

## ELECTRONIC NETS

*"But regulators may be dragging their feet on this issue."*

ROBERT SCHWARTZ *is a professor of finance at New York University and one of the nation's leading market theorists.*

There's certainly an ongoing argument in the financial industry over how to trade securities, and the computer has made that argument possible. But there's a broader question: What regulatory power ought the SEC exercise? Basically, there are two things the SEC does. It ensures that trading is fair and honest, and it exercises control over what market system is desirable. I think the SEC's first role is desirable. As an economist, I'm not nearly so certain about the other role—designing the structure of the industry. There's no doubt it does, but computers have made this kind of oversight increasingly complex.

The computer is a powerful force for change. Eventually orders will bypass both the dealers and physical exchanges like the NYSE. In fact, it's happening now. But regulators may be dragging their feet on this issue, with some of these computerized, electronic systems strangled at birth. Of course, it's not just regulators that are making it hard for people to start electronic exchanges, but the involvement of regulators can make it more difficult.

# FINANCIAL REGULATION
## ◆
### PROTECTIONISM

*"If we can't attract foreign issuers here,*
*the market will move away from us."*

GEORGE DOUGHERTY *is a vice president with the investment banking firm of Foley, Mufson, Howe & Co. He specializes in sales of restricted and control stock both domestically and internationally.*

The Securities Act of 1934 came into being after the Crash of 1929. Congress saw massive sales of bogus domestic and international stock in this country and decided then that no one could sell shares in the public market unless those shares are registered and the SEC has approved the sale.

But rules have changed somewhat since the old days. Now the SEC will allow the sale of some stock without registration once the company has done its original initial public offering and other conditions are met. The rule is 144, and it will let you sell in the public market.

Rule 144 pierced the barrier between holders of unregistered shares and the public. Recently, the SEC has done the same thing for foreign stocks that it did for domestic ones. Through Ruling 144a, foreign issuers can sell to qualified buyers without having to go through the usual SEC registration process.

But Rule 144a has not flooded the market with foreign stock. Europeans believe the regulations over here are horrible and that we require too much disclosure wrapped up in too much red tape.

As a country, we've always been insular. We're insular in our language especially, but there's no great pressure for us to reach out at the moment. This goes for finance too. Rule 144a hasn't significantly increased the flow of capital from the United States into foreign issues in our marketplace. That's too bad. If we can't attract foreign issuers here, the market will begin to move away from us.

---◆---

## DOMESTIC SOLUTIONS

*"We've done a plastering job, a patchwork job with our regulatory system."*

ALAN GART, *a former money manager and bank executive, is the author of seven books on finance, including* Regulation, Deregulation, Reregulation.

The basic problem that our financial industry faces is the large number of new products we've developed. What are the shortcomings of these new products? While derivative securities can be worthwhile investments in the hands of knowledgeable institutional players, there are enormous risks in some derivatives securities. These are synthetic products that are riskier than the old-fashioned products that have been around for a long time.

We've done a plastering job, a patchwork job with our regulatory system, but we haven't solved the fundamental problem: Some of our institutions—banks—are being penalized by over-regulation. There is no reason, for instance, why banks are restricted in where they can locate branches.

In the future it's going to be difficult to differentiate an insurance company, a bank, and a brokerage firm. Classic political lines have been drawn between these industries, and these regulatory barriers between industries have to be rethought. Regulation is supposed to provide safety and protection for investors, but it's not supposed to be punitive or restrictive. In this country, financial regulation arose because of public concerns about the safety of financial institutions and the security of people who purchased insurance, stocks, and bonds. The solutions of the past don't necessarily work today.

◆

## WORLDWIDE RISK

*"There is a glimmer of light in that there is certainly an improvement of the monitoring of risk."*

PAUL GIBSON *has been a top financial editor for both* Forbes *and* Financial World. *He recently summarized his experiences on* Wall Street *in the intriguingly titled book* Bear Trap: Why Wall Street Doesn't Work.

Few in the public and media realize how radically the financial securities industry has changed. There are three major forces—technology, globalization, and deregulation, all intertwining—and two minor ones—ethics and taxation—responsible for this. If you put them together, you find that Wall Street has moved entirely away from the approach of the customer's man.

Wall Street is something new—an industry that has reinvented itself with billions of dollars of capital for trading and underwriting purposes. But the public still trades stocks and bonds the old-fashioned way. Meanwhile, the professionals increasingly trade in huge blocks in whole regions of the world.

What also concerns me is the lemming-like approach in investing. It used to be a hot stock, but now we tell investors a story about a hot region. The result is the same. You'll be buying into a market just as the leaders are getting out. One of the problems here is that extraordinarily clever people are involved in the creation and the trading of these instruments. I'm not sure what will come first—regulation that tries to crack down or a major turndown that sparks efforts to reregulate. There is a glimmer of light in that there is certainly an improvement of the monitoring of risk with some of the new workstations and software packages. Professional investors can use the new technology to put in more controls. But whether they will be able to keep pace with the financial engineers is a question.

---◆---

## WORLDWIDE INFORMATION

*"Regulators are having more and more difficulty dealing with the new environment."*

NICOLA MEADEN *is the founder of London-based TASS Management Ltd., an international investment ranking service tracking performance of some of the most powerful international money funds in the derivatives and currency markets.*

The United States leads the world in rules and regulations put in place over the last 20 years. But regulations aren't international. I think the fact that they are different everywhere is bad business. And now with technology, regulations sometimes don't do what they're supposed to. The world is changing.

The derivatives industry is international, and in order to be competitive big investors need access to international markets. That's why having different regulatory environments in each market is frustrating, especially for international funds.

Very often managers will market a fund in only one country because it gets so complicated to do more than one or even to market to anything but an existing client base. And the reasons for all these regulations have to do with protecting the public. But who says it's more dangerous to the pocketbook to sell a futures fund than a Japanese warrant?

In the United States you're not allowed to pay performance fees if you invest in funds investing in stocks. It's part of your SEC regulations. That's why mutual funds get paid annual fees but no performance fees. But regulators are having more and more difficulty dealing with the new environment. First, there are all these new instruments. Second, even the central banks are having a hard time trying to control currency rates. It was marvelous when the currency traders started bashing the hell out of the Italian lira and then out of the sterling—you could finally see the power of the market and that governments and regulators could not dictate at the end of the day. That's certainly marketshock.

# CENTRAL BANKING

◆

## HISTORICAL OVERVIEW

### *"Restrictions in this country have made our banking system very weak."*

GEORGE SELGIN *is a respected free-market economist on the cutting edge of banking theory. His articles have appeared in numerous economic journals, as well as on* The Wall Street Journal's *editorial page.*

Central banks were not originally intended to help the economy. The Bank of England was set up to raise funds to pay for the war with France in the late 1600s. Central banks were fiscal devices initially. The monetary justifications for their existence came later. When they set up the Bank of England, the last thing they had in mind was the public good.

In this country, we've always distrusted the power of banking and as a result we've had too many banks—10,000 to 20,000 of them—and that's really perverse. If banks, that is, could open up anywhere and buy each other without countervening regulations, you'd have maybe 1,000 banks and maybe 50 to 100 truly national banks. These larger banks would perform securities functions performed by our investment banks and, especially, by Wall Street.

Restrictions in this country have made our banking system very weak. In Canada, not one bank failed during the Depression. Canada's system is like the European system, strong and diverse.

I favor private currency. The monopoly of currency by government is detrimental to the economy. I would like to see private banks take over the function of the Fed. The idea of banks issuing their own money sounds odd, but it's no odder than banks issuing credit cards or giving customers their own engraved checks.

I favor deregulating money and banks completely. That sounds radical, but one can pretty much predict what would arise in the absence of reserve banking. Singapore and Hong Kong are two of the few monetary systems left without central banks, and both have been good markets for investments.

The fact that these strong economies lack central banks speaks for itself. Both countries have managed to keep stable monies without central banks. It's true that the currencies are pegged to the dollar, but we're talking about choosing between evils in our current system, and the greater evil is the central bank itself.

---

## THE GOLD STANDARD

*"The government should be separated from money."*

JOE SALERNO *is associate professor of economics at the Lubin School of Business, Pace University.*

A gold standard eliminates inflation, especially if there is no fractional reserve banking. What we need is to have banks holding a 100 percent reserve so they can't lend out any more than what they can secure against. Otherwise they can play games.

A system like this would do away with the Federal Reserve. Right now, the Fed is legally permitted to write a check out of thin air—it can literally print money up, creating bank reserves. The ability to create money gives central bankers enormous power, but that doesn't mean they always use it right. The rate of growth of money being slow or too tight is what initially causes the business cycle downturn.

Recession starts in the capital goods industry, which is where recessions always begin, and then it trickles through to consumer goods. Eventually the Fed will manage to stimulate the economy again through lowering rates, and the cycle will begin once more. The Fed stimulus is the culprit for both boom and bust. If you go on stimulating, the swings become wilder and you get hyperinflation.

The government should be separated from money. A democratic government will always use its power to inflate the money supply. Deficit spending gets the votes, but it also increases taxes or results in inflation when the Fed borrows in the market to pay for those programs. But then the politicians will get scared of inflation and drive rates up faster, until a recession begins. Once you're in a recession, the Fed will lower rates further than they would have fallen normally and set off a boom. The boom will raise rates again, and in good times the politicians will start spending and borrowing. The cycle will repeat itself.

We need a country with strong property rights and a government that has responsible monetary policies that keep monetary growth low and the business cycle to a minimum. The current financial and legal complexity of our economics is uncalled for. The common law of England was the culmination of what we needed for a free society. That kind of approach to the law and a gold standard would be a recipe for a more prosperous society. What will it take to bring it about? An economic disaster. Only as things worsen will people look around and suggest reforms of our monetary system.

MURRAY ROTHBARD *is a former personal pupil of the famous founder of the Austrian school of economics, Ludwig von Mises, and a famous free-market economist and author in his own right. Rothbard teaches at the University of Nevada, Las Vegas.*

Since the 1930s prices have been going up steadily, whether there is a boom or not. Since countries came off the gold standard in the 1930s, in part due to the continued costs of World War I, there hasn't been any check on monetary expansion except the central banks' own will. Prices keep going up and up. They go up less in a recession than in a boom period, but they go up.

We saw the same pattern in Japan in the 1980s. The U.S. Fed put pressure on the Japanese to expand credit and to decrease savings rates—to inflate. If the United States expands credit and other countries don't, then our money depreciates over time. Maybe we wanted a little depreciation in the 1980s but not much.

During the 1920s and the 1980s, the establishment claimed that the boom was permanent, but any government stimulation will lead to unsound investments, and the longer a boom goes on, the worse it gets. Countries end up with inflated real estate markets just as we saw both here and in Japan, especially toward the end of a boom.

RON PAUL, *a former four-term congressman from Texas, knows the way the Washington money game is played. He served on the House Banking Committee before resuming his medical practice in the mid-1980s.*

Technology has helped us compensate for our unstable monetary system and has even allowed this system to last as long as it has. Technology continues to patch it together, but it won't last forever. Money originated as a commodity, and we've now allowed this fiat-money system to get way out of kilter.

Something will happen to put a crack in the wall. For years people have put up with currency fluctuation, but eventually confidence will erode, and some sort of gold standard will start to look promising again. A centralized currency can't possibly work—not even a European Monetary Union. The French will never succumb to the German central bankers and neither will the English.

I don't advocate locking the doors to the Fed, but I do say we

ought to legalize a competitive tender. If we're wrong, there is no
harm done. It's available and that's that.

———————◆———————

# HARD MONEY

## *"As a nation, we just don't have the requisite backbone to bear the pain to make it different."*

MARTHA EDEN *is the top trader for the Hanseatic Group, a Hot Money manager running funds for the Swiss-based Julius Baer Trust Company, among others.*

We live in a floating-currency environment where at least one
currency has to act like a hard currency—that is, as if it were
linked to a commodity. What are the properties of a commodity-
linked currency? Low inflation and steady interest rates are the
main ones. Just as important, the country behind the currency
has to command world confidence or the currency won't have
any liquidity. That's why the currency of Japan or Germany can't
emerge as the single hard currency in place of the dollar. There
are still lingering doubts about Germany and Japan. Both are
still tainted strongly by World War II, and I think many continue
to see them as racist, closed societies.

In terms of the currency itself, Germany has the most potential
as a world leader with a hard currency. By "hard" I mean a
currency that is strong and managed by a serious central banking
policy. In Germany, both politicians and central bankers care
that the currency stays strong. People in Germany understand
what it means to have a strong currency. We don't have any idea
in this country. Our structural inflation is like a jack-in-the-box.
As a nation, we just don't have the requisite backbone to bear

the pain to make it different. The budget and trade deficit are going to balloon, but our savings rate is still going down.

This budget crisis is nowhere near under control. When Clinton backed down on cost-of-living adjustments to social security, the game was over. If he had stayed with it, it would have meant he was serious about controlling costs, and the economy would have taken off.

It's inevitable there will be a period of consolidation. There will be more power in fewer hands. The markets will mandate the change. Something will happen—a marketshock. That's right. Something to bring them to their senses.

———————◆———————

## THE POWER STRUGGLE

*"The main concern of John Reed of Citicorp was overcontrol by the big European central banks—he thinks they have too much power already."*

KEITH HAZLEY *is head of trading for an Irish-managed opportunity fund. His speculations in currency forwards and options place him at the cutting edge of Hot Money finance.*

Almost all our funds trade in currencies, though we've also set up a bond fund. We're a hedge fund in the sense that our funds are called hedged. Basically we run a computer model that buys and sells currencies in such a way that the positions tend to hedge themselves.

We need to be careful in this volatile environment. The European Rate Mechanism (ERM) was never designed to be a platform for a single currency, only to be a platform to avoid large movements. The central banks would do the fine tuning, but they wouldn't try to go against the market. No one counted on the kind of recession that Europe underwent in the early 1990s—complicated by the German acquisition of East Germany and the inflation there. The Bundesbank cracked down on inflation just when France, England, and Italy needed lower rates to recover from recession.

Some U.S. bankers are worried about the way things are headed. I went to a presentation here in Dublin. The main concern of John Reed of Citicorp was overcontrol by the big European central banks—he thinks they have too much power already. He felt there was already too much power given to the Bundesbank, and he thinks the Fed has too much power too. Only when power is relinquished do reasonable economic policies arise.

Politicians want a single currency, even a single greater European state, and they'll vote for it even when the people don't. There've been examples of that already. There's a big power struggle going on between markets and authority.

# INTERNATIONAL INVESTING

$$\blacklozenge$$

## OVERVIEW

### *"Regulators have to realize that the world has changed."*

RICHARD KLITZBERG, *a former institutional broker for Bache & Co., has run a growing fund-of-funds operation since 1982. Princeton, New Jersey-based Klitzberg has grown up with the business, and he says his Klitzberg Associates' network of New Money managers extends around the globe.*

There are three kinds of international money. First is the money that goes abroad because it seeks anonymity. This kind of money is less performance-driven because its owners care more about keeping capital intact than they do about making stellar returns. They'll give their funds to a Swiss private banker who extracts 6 or 7 percent in fees and commissions and proceeds to invest it in safe, high-quality instruments that pay maybe a gross 10 percent or 11 percent return. But the investor is relieved because he's getting 3 percent or 4 percent on his money, and it hasn't been dissipated. Most important, he can maintain his anonymity.

Second is the money that's attracted to mutual and private funds, in either this country or in big overseas outfits like Global Asset Management (GAM). Often firms like GAM start out running one family's money. They may operate like a fund of funds, seeking out fund managers in various countries. GAM started this way, but now it offers a series of funds to English and international investors, mostly high-net-worth investors. England has what we would consider a mutual fund industry but it's not as large as ours, and it tends to attract a wealthier clientele. There are other famous fund groups abroad besides GAM, especially some famous Swiss ones like Hausmann Holdings and Leveraged Capital Holdings.

Finally there's the really aggressive money. This is money that seeks the best return all over the world, but it's never clear whether those gains are realized or whether there's any serious discipline behind the investing.

That's the international investment scene minus the pension plans and institutional money. Now most of that money is invested locally. Canada, for instance, has a law that certain institutional money can only be invested 10 percent outside of the country, and most of Germany's money is invested in Germany. In this country we don't have rules against investing outside the United States, but we do have something called the Rules of Prudence, which say that you have to manage other people's money as if it were your own. These Rules of Prudence date back to the 1700s, when they were first formulated and have been updated through the Employment Retirement Income Security

Act (ERISA) and other kinds of regulations. Of course, Rules of Prudence aren't really a set of rules in the formal sense. They're actually common law, a series of historic decisions that gave direction to fiduciaries managing other people's money. However, in this country as elsewhere, things are changing rapidly. It could be our Rules of Prudence need updating. Rules of Prudence tend to get updated in bad markets.

I run a fund of funds. I set up partnerships for individuals and institutions, and then I find managers to run the money. Most of these are what you would call hedge fund managers. They can run funds in which they will invest both long and short, diminishing risk. But hedge funds certainly don't do this all the time. They'll go long or short for profit purposes, or they'll invest in options or bonds. There's really no limit on what a hedge fund can do so long as it's investing in a securitized product. Right now the small investor can invest in about 4,000 mutual funds, all of which are doing pretty much the same thing the same way. Many of these funds have gone up because the market has gone up. But I can remember coming into this business in the 1960s, and I remember the market moving down from 1969 to 1974, until it sloughed off billions of dollars. The same thing will happen sooner or later. All those investors who think that mutual funds are like a savings account will gradually see their investments erode a little bit at a time. That's the danger—that it will start and keep going. It may be a marketshock that sets the cycle going, but what is so dangerous is that it will continue.

Regulators have to realize that the world has changed. They're going to have to let investors in on something besides naked long stocks. In the next 25 years, investors will have to be invested in different instruments and different markets, both here and abroad. They'll have to use hedging techniques including margin and options. They'll have to sell short as well as go long. Most important, they'll have to diversify, and they'll have to do it fast. Mutual funds would be good vehicles for investors of the future, but only if they're given more flexibility—and encouraged to utilize that flexibility.

ROGER IBBOTSON *is professor of finance at the Yale School of Management. He is also president of Ibbotson Associates, a Chicago-based consulting firm pioneering international analytics and quantitative data.*

The barriers are breaking down. It's easier and easier to invest globally, and there are direct ways to invest. Quantitative investing has come a long way over the last 10 to 20 years. Most of the techniques were developed over the last 30 years and applied in the last 10 years.

Fixed income is almost solely quantitative, in that an investment in fixed income is a promise to pay you back at some time horizon and in some currency, so there is a purely quantitative contract—one that you can use to quantify risk and return mathematically.

We've already had an equity explosion too, internationally, though it's harder to quantify and it has been slower to take place. Still, most equities are bought by domestic investors. My position is that country matters and industry matters and that you better know the various macroeconomic factors. The specific stock matters, too, but not so much by the time it's put into a portfolio.

Futures and options markets have also seen terrific growth internationally. Futures are an easy way to buy and sell whole markets with low transaction costs, and of course there are futures in stocks and bonds as well as currencies. Trading in financial futures is larger than the trading in the underlying market. Commodities do better in a high-inflation environment. The key to investing is anticipating and deciding where markets might go and deciding if that's where you want to go.

———————◆———————

## THE PLAYERS

### *"The United States has the opportunity to blow the world away if it moves quickly."*

MARK ADORIAN *is part owner of Micropal, an industry-leading, international data firm supplying prices and information on 20,000 public and private funds worldwide.*

There are basically 3,500 offshore funds, domiciled in offshore havens such as Dublin, Bermuda, Hong Kong and the Bahamas. There are 10 or 11 domiciles in all. Most public funds are head-quartered in the country where they do business and conform to the U.S. domestic structure—that is, they look a lot like U.S. mutual funds.

If you take a positively correlated fund together with a nega-tively correlated fund, you will increase your reward without increasing risk. You are better off with more assets allocated than less. People don't understand you can take more risk if you are more diversified. I invest in offshore funds, and some of these funds' investments are risky but others are quite safe, so I get to be very daring without increasing my risk substantially. I get a turbocharged return.

There is nothing to prevent a U.S. citizen from buying an offshore fund, though people often think there is. What stops most people, of course, is the minimum. You often have to be quite well-off to afford an offshore fund. Still, those who can afford it, especially Americans, are shoving money into these funds.

Eventually U.S. groups will set up shops overseas and products will be purchased by U.S. investors, so the sooner the regulators permit a variety of funds, the better. The United States has the opportunity to blow the world away if it moves quickly. U.S. public funds can market around the world if the regulators let them. But U.S. regulators are still concerned that the investor will get fleeced if certain controls are removed. It will take time in my view.

JOHAN SEGERDAHL *runs international investing and institutional sales, including international trading, for Chicago Corp.*

It's no secret that some of the most attractive investments can be found overseas. There are people everywhere wondering whether they ought to be diversified a little more. The British have been putting money offshore for years, but proportionally, the American investor has not put as much money abroad. I believe it's less than 5 percent now. In Great Britain, the individual is diversified at about 15 to 20 percent. The big institutions investing people's cash are typically the big insurers and banks over there.

The big, private European banks have subsidiaries that are brokers here, and they specialize in recommending foreign stocks. Then there are securities firms that specialize in selling foreign stocks like Crosby Securities, which specializes in Hong Kong stock.

The technology today is moving everything toward globalization. We're now able to see prices instantaneously. From a regulatory perspective, I can understand how scary this is becoming. It used to be a rule book with a small club, and now you've got all these new investors who can play. There's no way for governments to keep control, unless all the governments try to get together.

We're going through a period of liberation. I come from Sweden. It was a socialist state when I was growing up, and it still is in many ways. They put up capital limitations, and they thought this was a way to protect their currency, but that never works. The cycle is turning.

---◆---

## DIVERSIFICATION

### *"There is going to be a great deal more volatility to come."*

LEWIS ALTFEST *is a financial planning consultant with a lifelong interest in international investing.*

Countries used to march in lockstep, but now international economic policies seem to be breaking down. We're in a new fiscal situation, and it is not appropriate to look at past volatility for patterns that might occur in the future. There is going to be a great deal more volatility to come, and funds that are hedged with currencies and other kinds of instruments will have their place in the investing panorama. For mutual funds, currency hedging is something they will have to handle with care and skill.

The benefits of international investing include investments that have little correlation with the U.S. marketplace. That's the main reason to diversify. Most investors would feel comfortable in a diversified country fund. Some of these are regional in the sense that they are European- or Pacific Basin-oriented. And the most diversified are the global ones.

A person who's young and wants to be invested fairly aggressively in stocks should have up to 20 percent of his or her whole portfolios overseas.

---◆---

## ASSET ALLOCATION AND TIMING

### *"The economy has been on the side of Wall Street."*

STEPHEN LEEB *is a business writer and editor of* Personal Finance, *an investment advisory publication.*

Stock markets run on empty and die on full, the exact opposite of a car. When there is a lot of slack in the economy, markets tend to do fine. If the economy is tight, stock markets won't do so well. The early 1990s were anomalous in that economies around the world remained slack for a long time. The financial system was basically a sponge for liquidity.

The financial system was in bad shape in 1990, and even banks like Citicorp were tottering, so the Fed had to provide an unprecedented amount of liquidity, and liquidity was just sopped up. Instead of making loans, banks just bought securities and put that money on their balance sheet. But I think we have reached the point at which banks are reliquified and appear to be loaning money again. This means the stock market will begin to tighten.

Investors who want to readjust their portfolios might look to commodities indexes to see whether prices are inflating and also at the commodity price and consumer price indexes. Other indicators are interest rates and unemployment rates. They give signs whether the economy, and therefore inflation, are gaining strength.

In the stock market itself investors can look at dividend/yield, which may be a more precise indicator now than price/earnings. The dividend/yield is the ratio between what a stock is selling for and what it is paying out in dividends based on earnings.

I foresee markets getting back to their more normal behavior in what will amount to a tighter market—a choppier stock market.

The economy has been on the side of Wall Street in the early 1990s, but the next two or three years of our economy will be characterized by more rapid growth, and therefore stocks will be more volatile than they have been.

Investors should use common sense when the economy is heating up. Money will find its way into industrial inventories,
homes, commodities, and metals. These are the investments that
consumers should be looking at diversifying into—perhaps international investments as well, not because of inflation but because
there's more opportunity internationally than in the United
States.

JOHN VAN ECK *is the founder of one of the country's largest and most
successful gold funds.*

Nobody can predict the price of gold day-to-day or year-to-year.
Gold prices tend to move in 4- to 10-year cycles. In the 1980s
gold moved down, and we got out, but we got back in too soon.
We never expected it to move down for so long.

Since no one can predict the price of gold, we buy it not to
make a play but to diversify. The government's tax-rate increase
coupled with the currency fluctuations in Europe and the weaken-
ing dollar make it important that the investor have some sort of
metals hedge in addition to other investments. Gold is a very
good hedge. It tends to be a countercyclical investment, doing
better when the stock and bond markets do worse. If you accept
that the democracies have a hard time controlling themselves,
then easy money and eventual tightening lie ahead for Europe
and America.

These constitute the cyclical business swings that von Mises
spoke about. I studied with von Mises, and that's when I determined to change my mutual fund to a fund that invested in gold.
Von Mises pointed out the tendency of governments to expand
credit excessively. It is impossible to predict what central bankers
will do with monetary policy—when debt burdens have become
excessive, when inflationary expectations suddenly change—and
how investors and markets will behave. That's why you don't
buy gold to make an immediate killing. Only speculators do

that. Investors will include gold as a part of their portfolio—
perhaps 5 to 10 percent. When other parts of their investments
go down, chances are the rise in gold prices will make up for it.

———————◆———————

## DEFLATION AND REFLATION

### *"The low interest rates create an economic distortion."*

VICTOR SPERANDEO, *whose writings are often found in* Barron's, *is one of the top traders in the business and the founder of Rand Management.*

Here's a review of what happened in this country in the last 10
years, starting with the 1986 tax act. In 1986, the tax act was
a good idea. President Reagan attempted to make investments
more efficient by eliminating tax shelters. But when he elimi-
nated a lot of tax deductions in certain areas of tax shelters—
real estate—the accompanying decline in values brought on the
S&L crisis. When you take away a great advantage, it's going to
have consequences. In addition, all these shelters were business
generators.

The stock market benefited from the tax act. Before 1986,
real estate was the place to be because people thought inflation
was going to come back sooner or later, and the tax advantages
were fantastic. We all remember what happened in 1987. The
market went up, the Fed tightened and the market crashed. Then
the Fed panicked, and the market reversed after the Fed eased.

Now we come to the Bush administration. George Bush was
nothing more than a moderate Democrat—a do-nothing, wishy-
washy kind of guy. He signed the Clean Air Act and instituted
tax increases in exchange for spending cuts that didn't happen.
This caused a further collapse in the economy. In addition, the
regulations he put in caused a collapse in employment. Business

didn't want to hire. The Disabilities Act, the Clean Air Act—
every one of those acts hurt. We're in a deflationary period now,
with major corporations laying off. So what does the Fed do?
Lower interest rates. That increases demand for money and re-
duces supply.

The banks are borrowing the money, but they don't want to
loan to the public because they can loan to the government by
buying Treasury bonds. So they're borrowing from the Fed and
paying a low interest rate and then turning around and lending
to Treasury at a high one. Also, the low interest rates create an
economic distortion. Money is flowing into the stock market
because savers have nowhere else to turn, and the stock market
goes up fast, so after a point, people are speculating since values
are overpriced. So what did the Fed accomplish? A surge of
speculation that robbed new business of capital and slowed real
increases of productivity that the progressives are so eager to
promote.

Normal productivity comes about when you keep your work
force and let them gradually build up production. Employment
generally grows with productivity. Today, layoffs and plant
closings are causing a lack of supply, which will eventually
cause price increases. However, now we're in a deflationary
mode that may continue for some time. We'll experience further slow growth without price increases until the Clinton
administration realizes it's failed. Then it will promote further
interest rate cuts, which will bring back inflation and cause
another crash.

## WHAT I LEARNED

◆

Our financial system is composed of industry classes: insurance,
banking (itself divvied up) and securities sales and trading. Top

banker Walter Wriston has analyzed how the information revolution is breaking down these industry classes, but the players in the financial industry with the most to lose, as well as the regulators who watch over the various segments of the financial industry, will no doubt continue to fight against change. As a result, investors will be exposed to marketshocks as new economic tools collide with old-fashioned methods of doing business. Wall Street trader Gregg Kipnis says the first of the new-wave marketshocks was seen in the precipitous decline of the stock market in 1987. Stocks, as an investment, were weakened by rising interest rates. Then, says Big Money manager Bob Kirby, the physical-exchange system, embodied by the NYSE, was undermined by Wall Street firms and proprietary trading firms which used computers to track and manipulate order flow.

My insiders understand how exchange trading of all kinds is evolving. Electronic market maker Cary Grant and securities economist Robert Schwartz reinforced my conclusions about our current market system. The myths of the market—that a physical exchange system is necessary to centralize order flow, that specialists are necessary to an orderly market, that only a physical exchange system run by a self-regulatory organization and supervised by the SEC can harness the power of securities trading— collided with the reality of electronic trading in 1987. The reverberations are still being felt.

In 1992 and 1993, Wriston says, central bankers collided with foreign exchange specialists, and the traders temporarily won. As a result, central bankers had to revise their policies. Instead of trying to stick to predetermined ranges for interest rates, central bankers were forced to lower rates. Traders kept bidding weak currencies down, and central banks in England, Spain, and ultimately France finally were forced to accept lower rates. In both 1987 and 1992, regulators faced off with traders using electronic systems, and the result was a destabilization of the market.

While there can be no saying what market will be affected
next, my insiders seem to agree that some lessons can be drawn
from recent financial history. First, many marketshocks don't
just happen. They are the result of prolonged industry infighting
in which regulatory and business interests reinforce an unpalatable
system, which is then undermined by electronic trading. The
trigger to a marketshock sometimes appears to be regulatory in
nature. In 1987, the trigger was rising interest rates, as top New
Money trader Victor Sperandeo points out. In 1992, the trigger
was the increasing rigidity with which central bankers clung to
ERM rates. In 1995, who knows what it will be?

"Speculators" are often blamed for marketshocks. Regulators
and politicians tend to point to the private sector when casting
blame for what has gone wrong. But the sophisticated investor—
the "new" investor, as different as the new money manager is from
the old—will understand the truth and try to protect himself or
herself in the best way possible.

How can investors protect themselves from continued marketshocks? Famous economist Murray Rothbard and former congressman Ron Paul depressed me with their hard-headed realism
about how tough solutions are.

It's difficult to argue against their conclusions that in a fiat-
money system there are limited choices and that the global economy will continue to grind down unless we exercise some harsh
discipline at home and abroad—perhaps even moving toward a
fully realized gold standard again. (Of course, my Austrian insiders would hasten to point out that the "moving" probably won't
be done by governmental decree but by individuals who gradually
come to distrust our delinked system of paper money and turn
to gold as the preferred substitute.)

Still, barring the near-term collapse of worldwide mercantilism, the international fiat-money system will continue to hold
sway for the foreseeable future—and investors must deal with it

as it is. Certainly there is hope for hard-headed, economically literate investors who understand modern market cycles and the power of appropriate diversification. The rest of this book examines what these investors might do to mitigate risks of the information age's collision with the regulatory age.

# INVESTMENT SUMMARY
## MARKETSHOCK: DEFINITION OF THE PROBLEM

♦ Marketshocks can be short and sharp, or long and grinding. Sometimes they are the result of international or domestic political or economic events—a war, an embargo, a bad harvest. But increasingly the collision of regulation and information may generate marketshocks. This kind of marketshock occurs when rigid economic instruments and exchange systems collide with new forms of electronic investment and screen trading.

♦ Marketshock can be predicted though not necessarily timed. When a market or business cycle is reaching a cyclical top or when regulators impose new rules on expanding asset classes and investment strategies, look for a marketshock.

♦ Marketshock is not a modern anomaly but our modern-day fiat-money system makes marketshocks more likely. The collision of banking and financial regulation with the marketplace (and new technologies like telegraphs and telephones) has likely always produced marketshocks. The advent of electronic financial mechanisms—computers and data-delivery systems—has increased this phenomenon's velocity and power.

## WHAT THE INVESTOR CAN DO

- Understand that the rules of investment instruments are developed not only by the marketplace but also by dominant industry players.
- Be aware of how government and industry actions can affect investments and make plans accordingly—to protect assets from deflation, or disinflation, and reflation and to anticipate marketshock.
- Diversify, not only by investing in several different kinds of securities but by investing with different vehicles in different financial sectors.

## CHAPTER TWO

# REGIONS

◆

## What's Hot, What's Not, Around the World

Once readers have internalized the idea of what a marketshock is, they are ready to figure out what to do next. We've already dealt a little bit with allocation via the business cycle, and we'll be coming back to it, but this chapter focuses on international diversification across regions. More and more, economic cycles worldwide operate in sync; still, some countries are more hospitable to investments, especially securitized investments, than others.

An investor seeking to diversify fully must understand the regions of the world that offer the most promise and least problems and understand what builds successful economies. There is a fundamental and ongoing struggle occurring between government and the markets it regulates, so investors are probably going to seek out the markets where government is least involved in basic commerce.

What builds healthy economies? Most non-Keynesian economists would probably agree that the basics involve low, steady interest rates, modest taxes, and high savings rates. The money pros I spoke to tend to look for these signals—along with respect for property rights—in the countries where they want to invest.

How does our domestic economy stack up in these areas? Not very well, say the top economists I interviewed for this book. Mark Skousen, adjunct professor of economics at Rollins College and author of numerous provocative books on economics, is quick to identify the importance of fundamental principles of healthy economies, but on several of these issues, the United States virtually flunks. This country's savings rate is higher than it was in the 1980s—about 4 percent versus 3 percent—but this pales in comparison to some of the double-digit savings and investment rates put up by countries like Hong Kong and Singapore.

Warburg International vice president James Donald also is a proponent of high savings rates and low interest rates. Donald, who helps supervise a European country fund, looks for high savings rates and a stable monetary policy among the countries his fund invests in. Because of Europe's wrenching recession, he doesn't see any high flyers in the immediate future.

Japan may have plans to influence Pacific Rim countries, but U.S. perceptions of Japan may be wrong. If we look closely, we'll see the Japanese success during the mid- to late 20th century has been built on small, cumulative, intelligent decisions. The true Japanese miracle probably lies in the country's high savings rates and modest interest rates. Marry that to relatively low taxes, and you have the real explanation for Japan's success—not the workings of hyperintelligent and farsighted bureaucrats.

The miracle of Japan is echoed by other regions in the area— China, Hong Kong, Singapore, Taiwan. All may see increasing growth in the 1990s, in part because of free market reforms or because the necessary ingredients—low interest rates, high savings rates—are already present within the countries. The same may hold true in South America. In Africa, according to American University economist George Ayittey, "despite difficulties, some countries are managing to do well—Botswana and Zimbabwe among them." Ayittey says that Africans' problems have been blamed on the West for too long. "There's a new generation," he says. "The new generation wants to dismantle the whole state-controlled structure. In the long term Africa has a lot of promise."

Ayittey explains well what is happening in Africa, but it is more difficult to find someone who is sure what is happening in Central Europe and the former Soviet Union. One of the more eloquent and disturbing perspectives I came in contact with while finishing this book was an article by famed financier George Soros. In the October 7, 1993, issue of the *New York Review of Books*, Soros makes the point that the United States' lack of action in opposing the ethnic cleansing of the Bosnian Muslims has created a terrible precedent. Writes Soros, "Bosnia demonstrates once again that borders can be changed by force and that this will be accepted internationally." Soros thinks that Bosnia's example won't be wasted on other strongmen and thugs whose Marxist backgrounds make Central Europe an especially volatile breeding ground of power politics. As I write, the war in Bosnia is still not resolved, and civil wars either flicker or blaze throughout the region. The biggest question of all is the eventual stability of the former Soviet Union, something no one can predict.

It is a risky business to forecast political events any more than economic ones. Countries in South America, Asia, and Eastern Europe are in flux. But short of an international blow-up, it would seem that today's judicious international investing harbors at least a little more promise than in the past for the informed and well-advised investor.

---◆---

## RISK OVERVIEW

*"The idea that you have to liberalize the political system to reform your economy is not necessarily true."*

BILL COPLIN *is a professor at the Maxwell School, Syracuse University, and cofounder of an international risk forecasting group, Political Risk Services, which is owned by London-based IBC.*

Around the world there are three basic economies: the First World economies, the Tigers who are racing ahead and, finally, in Africa and a few other places in the world, people who are still exceedingly poor.

Among the problems that impede growth internationally, the primary one is corruption, and it's hard to address. Sometimes the journalists and business community will make it out to be worse than it is. Tiananmen Square caused a drop in the value of Hong Kong currency, but two months later the currency came back to where it was. The Chinese government has always vacillated between economic liberalism and Marxist policies. While you need a stable political environment for reform, the idea that you have to liberalize the political system to reform your economy is not necessarily true.

Another good example is Chile, one of the best economies in Latin America. Pinochet ran it like a dictatorship. Brazil, by contrast, is a mess because it couldn't maintain reform. Egypt is an interesting country. It is stable but can't get moving.

The biggest economic problem I see is the factionalized, weak political system worldwide. The answer isn't democracy per se but in growth with low inflation—increasing production and development.

---◆---

## INVESTMENT OVERVIEW

### *"Encourage supply, not demand."*

MARK SKOUSEN, *a financial economist and author, is well-known for his acute analysis of financial affairs. He is adjunct professor of economics and finance at Rollins College, Winter Park, Florida.*

The United States has one of the highest capital gains tax rates in the world. A survey I did showed that over half the major countries in the world have no capital gains tax. But look at the rate of return in countries that have developed stock markets. The track record is considerably better among major countries that have no capital gains tax than those that do. In countries without capital gains taxes, the economy is growing faster and the stock market rate of return is growing faster. Rate of savings is extremely important too. The Asians, with their emphasis on thrift, have pretty high savings rates. However, we must be aware of countries like Singapore with an industrial policy of forced savings. It has the highest investment rate in the world— 40 percent. In comparison, Hong Kong has an 8 percent growth rate with an investment rate of 20 percent. Yet Hong Kong and Singapore are averaging the same growth rate, so a high savings and investment rate is not a panacea.

Some countries maintain a stable anti-inflation policy at all times. Switzerland comes the closest in this regard. Domestically, despite what some people might think, Switzerland has a strong free-market bias, with much of the decision-making power at the canton or local level. I've been recommending Swiss stocks, bonds, and currencies for some time now. A 10,000-Swiss-franc investment in 1969 would be worth 100,000 today, and that's in a very conservative environment.

A lot of countries, especially in Asia and Latin America, are starting to think about a model that more closely resembles the supply-side model: Encourage supply, not demand; encourage technology, the expansion of capital, and the expansion of the savings rate rather than consumption; don't worry about consumption. The countries adopting these models, specifically, the Asian countries, are catching up with the United States. That's the future of economics.

———————◆———————

## EMERGING MARKETS

### "Developing countries' economies are expected to grow a lot more quickly than developed markets."

IAN WILSON *runs an emerging-markets funds publication for Micropal.*

Emerging markets are exploding. An investor who invested 20 percent in emerging markets and 80 percent in domestic funds would have added considerably to his or her profits over the last few years without upping the risk. Sometimes international investing can actually lower risk since there are countries that are negatively correlated to Europe and America's business cycle. India is negatively correlated because historically it's been virtually closed to foreign investors, so the ripple effect of the business cyle doesn't include it yet. Investors who want that kind of negative correlation should seek out countries that haven't come into the mainstream of the world economy.

Developing countries' economies are expected to grow a lot more quickly than developed markets—at some 6 percent to 12 percent in the 1990s. The high end would be China, where some of the provinces are growing rapidly, and Hong Kong too. That kind of growth compares with 1, 2, or 3 percent growth in Canada and the United States.

For investors, the most expensive way of investing in foreign countries is probably to buy stock there. They can always try to go through a broker based in the country where they want to invest, but it's probably easier to find a country fund or a regional fund.

---◆---

# EUROPE

## *"Down the road there are major monetary and political trends that lead toward a union."*

JAMES DONALD *is treasurer of the Europe Fund managed by Warburg Investment Management, a subsidiary of the powerful old-line London-based bank Warburg.*

In 1994, Continental Europe's economies are going to rebound. If I were to separate out individual countries, I would say that East Germany is more promising than Germany proper. We're playing East Germany with the East German Investment Trust, which invests in various private enterprises throughout the country.

France's economy will recover in 1994. We see a reasonably strong recovery and prefer some of the smaller companies in the stock market. In Spain, the socialist government has won another victory and now will have to figure out what to do about government spending, which has exploded. There is good potential in Spain if they can control the budget. In the United Kingdom, we're expecting a major resurgence in 1994—a big bounce-back from a very severe recession.

In Italy the market has been strong but there are a fairly limited number of stocks to buy. There may be a more vigorous economy, depending on how the political turmoil works out. The problem in Italy, as in Spain, is the budget deficit, which is so big the government hasn't been paying it down, just paying off the interest. But it's a drag on the economy and has to be brought down.

We like Switzerland very much. It's politically and economically stable with some huge international companies, including some worldwide pharmaceuticals and banks.

We don't anticipate that the European Community will crack up as some people believe. There will be a continued movement toward a federal Europe, though at this point it's a belief more than a fact. Down the road there are major monetary and political trends that lead toward a union.

---◆---

## EASTERN EUROPE AND RUSSIA

### *"This forecast assumes Russia stays on track."*

ERNEST STALZER *is managing director of International Financial Data Ltd., a Boston-based firm that covers 40 world markets through both publications and consulting.*

From an economic standpoint, this region is not nearly so dynamic as the Asian rim. At the end of 1993, budget deficits and inflation were quite high in Eastern Europe. Unemployment in Hungary, Poland, and Slovakia were over 13 percent, and inflation averaged over 20 percent. Poland comes closest to a free market, but on the whole these markets tend to be closed. You can't easily invest in them even if you wanted to. The markets are also very small. They have seen price appreciation, and some may already be overvalued.

There are some broad themes to the development of Eastern Europe. An engine of growth in all of them is an improvement of infrastructure after ownership issues and privatization are worked through. Infrastructure repairs could be worth billions. Telephones are antiquated and so are roads. Eastern Europe is linked to Germany and Austria, but new roads should offer other linkages as well. Eastern European companies offer investments for the long-term institutional investor at the moment. The private retail money will come later.

This forecast assumes that the former Soviet Union stays on track and continues to make progress toward democracy. The emergence of a government hostile to the West would put a big damper on the growth of Eastern European markets and maybe even reverse progress.

◆

## JAPAN

### *"It's hard to believe that there isn't some magic involved."*

KARL ZINSMEISTER, *a top international economic observer and fellow at the Washington-based American Enterprise Institute, is author of, among other papers,* Japan's Industrial Policy Doesn't Work.

Japanese management in the private and public realm has been quite competent on the whole, but the bubble economy was basically a misjudgment. It has made mistakes, especially in the area of selecting and supporting individual companies. In fact, the government has done more harm than good in industrial policy, a conclusion based on various Japanese studies. These failures aren't ordinarily noted in the press.

There has clearly been management success in Japan, and it has been so striking that it's hard to believe that there isn't some magic involved. The idea that this is built on lots of sweat and small, cumulative, intelligent decisions is difficult to believe. If it isn't this magical government-private sector cooperation, then what is it? Maybe they're just doing something better than us. That's the most frightening possibility of all—that they manage better, operate better, pay attention to the bottom line better.

The view that it's the government-private partnership that's making Japan tick is being propagated by Japan's bureaucrats. They're the people Washington talks to when they want an answer. You can't call a Japanese businessperson—they're secretive, usually speak only Japanese, and are not likely to be very well-informed about the trends of society. If you talk to the Japanese bureaucrats, they'll take the credit for the way Japan works. It's been my strong impression that American advocates of these private-public partnerships tend to come out of academia or law and tend not to have strong business backgrounds. They have an appealing message that fits hand-in-glove with a longtime agenda on the left, which has been to increase control of the economy by government. They ignore the fundamental strengths of Japan—its savings rates and stable economic policies.

**MARK SKOUSEN** (*see page* 76)

In the past, Japan has been a good international investment, though the Japanese government's control of industrial policy would seem to contradict much of what free-market economists believe in. But what people think about Japan may not be true. I believe the secret to the Japanese system is the adoption of American management techniques to emphasize quality at cheaper prices. Also, the government was active in encouraging export and savings. Until recently the country had virtually no capital gains tax.

There are two reasons why the Japanese real estate and stock market collapsed. One was the institution of a tight money policy that followed an inflationary policy and led them to adopt a standard Western Keynesian boom-bust cycle. Second, they imposed a capital gains tax, and that certainly hurt the market.

What people fail to understand is that the Japanese success story has to do with the amount of decision-making power at the level of the Japanese industrialists who look to what consumers want. The managed part of the economy is just not that significant.

◆

# PACIFIC RIM

## *"Hong Kong is a great way to make a China play."*

HELEN YOUNG-HAYES *manages $850 million in domestic and international funds for Janus Capital. Born in California, a first-generation Chinese-American, Young-Hayes speaks Mandarin.*

I believe we'll see big growth in China—maybe 13 percent a year. Look at the policies that are in place. In the mid- to late-1980s, China largely kept to itself, but it was clear that the state was bankrupting the government. Eventually the government took the agricultural economy off an allocation-based system and decentralized. It said, in effect, "You're your own boss, you can keep your profits." People did, and profits exploded. That was the first change, and since this experiment worked, they moved it elsewhere. In fact, China is the fastest-growing economy in the world.

We're invested in China through Hong Kong, through companies that derive profits in China, but we haven't overcommitted since I have concerns. There could be hiccups along the way. The economy has tended to grow at a very rapid pace for a few years, and eventually inflation will kick up and they'll have to slow things down, which they're starting to do.

But the reforms won't stop. The programs China is pursuing will continue even when the current leadership changes. The people are in favor of the reforms. The average Chinese citizen is asking, "Is my life getting better?" The answer is yes. They actually have much more freedom than five years ago—more freedom of speech for example—and on the whole there is much less paranoia throughout the society.

Hong Kong is going to benefit from China's pursuit of free

markets. For many Hong Kong companies, China is the primary market, and with China growing at such a rapid pace, Hong Kong is a great way to make a China play. I also think the recent rapprochement between Taiwan and China is historic. All the parties will be winners.

———————◆———————

## SOUTH AMERICA

*"You have a situation in this region that we think is extremely promising."*

SALVADORE DIAZ VERSON, *Cuban by birth, has retained a deep interest in South America and its prospects for success. After a short stint on Wall Street, he joined American Family Life and eventually became president. After fourteen years he left to start his own firm, Diaz-Verson Capital Investments.*

Many of our assets are south of the border in what I call first-tier South American countries: Mexico, Argentina, Venezuela, and Chile. A second tier of countries in which we are also invested or thinking of investing in includes Peru, Colombia, Jamaica, and Brazil.

There is a third tier we have hopes for in the future: Costa Rica and Trinidad and Tobago. Finally there are countries like Guatemala, Panama, and Cuba, where investment is impossible or there has to be more government stability. In this last group, the markets are still closed, and accounting standards have not been established. It is hard to evaluate companies with no accounting standards and few historical data.

People in these third-tier countries have realized that to grow and become part of the international financial system, they need stability and a democratic system. A lot of the top politicians in these countries have been educated in the United States and understand what to do to manage a country. The fall of communism has made it possible for countries to start to play on an international basis without having to worry about other political forces.

The second tier of South America may have the most potential in the long run. Colombia, with its drug cartel, is still unstable. In Peru the Shining Path's destabilizing impact is being diminished. Brazil continues to have very serious problems, chief among them inflation. It has had six ministers of finance in two years, so there's little continuity of policy. The Congress in Brazil is going to have to make a commitment to take control of interest rates and get inflation under control by cutting deficit spending.

In South America, companies I like include those in the banking and infrastructure industry. Most of the banks have good assets and have used the old way of banking—they don't finance long-term debt with short-term deposits and usually invest in things they know about in their own country. Because of a very young population, with good savings rates and increasingly disposable income, the situation in this region is extremely promising.

———————◆———————

## AFRICA

## *"In the long term, Africa has a lot of promise."*

GEORGE AYITTEY *is an associate professor at American University and the author of two books on African economics and finance. One of Africa's bright, young economic stars—and president of the Free Africa Foundation to establish African free markets—Ayittey knows as well as anyone else the vast potential of the world's richest continent.*

The ability of Africa to attract funds has been rather disappointing, and foreign investment has not found Africa to be an attractive place. The climate is hostile to foreign investment for several reasons. The first is a holdover from the colonial era—a misconception that because colonialists exploited and oppressed African people, there was a danger that foreign companies might continue that oppression. After independence many foreign companies were nationalized and taken over by the government. The private sector was severely regulated in its operations.

In addition, regulations or controls against repatriation of dividends or profits from Africa, high taxes on profits made by outside companies, and regulations on hiring practices contribute to make Africa a difficult place to invest in, let alone make money in. To attract foreign investment, most of these regulations will have to be removed, but African governments have been dragging their feet. One of the main reasons why the environment is not conducive to foreign investment is African governments' continued hostility to capitalism because it is identified with colonialism.

Yet Africa had free markets, free enterprise, and free trade long before colonial powers arrived. It's part of Africa's heritage. In a book on indigenous African institutions, I pointed out that there were marketplaces all over West Africa, for example, and these market activities were dominated by women, and are still today. Timbuktu was one great big market town. Kano in Nigeria and Mombasa in Kenya were linked by free-trade routes along which goods and people moved freely. Prices were not fixed in these markets or on these trade routes by tribal governments or African chiefs. The prices were determined by bargaining, which is still true today.

Some countries in Africa are in better shape than others. Nigeria adopted a federal system while countries like Tanzania and Ghana went socialist. Mauritius, Botswana, Ivory Coast, and The Gambia are more open to market economies because their leaders did not believe in socialism. The common problem is that regimes have concentrated a great deal of economic and political power in the hands of the state.

The ultimate solution for South Africa—and all of Africa—is to have a system in which no individual or party can capture the state. Power, that is, has to be taken away from the state and given back to people. When that happens, there will be a rise of market economies, decentralization, and a political system of the federal or confederate type. The African heritage is not based on statism. There were great empires in Africa based on the principal of confederation—a system with less power at the center and more power with constituent states. For a long time, the mess in Africa has been blamed by Africans on the West. A new generation of Africans is putting more emphasis on internal problems. They are insisting that reform should be internally generated and that Africa should clean up itself. This new generation wants to dismantle the whole state-controlled structure. In the long term, Africa has a lot of promise.

———————◆———————

## AMERICA FIRST

### *"The nature of the stock business is to baffle with bullshit."*

RICHARD SCHMIDT, *president of Stellar Management, is a Naples, Florida, money manager and the author of a monthly newsletter*, Risk Report.

The nature of the stock business is to baffle with bullshit—to convince people they're novices. That gives the institution and brokers a position of control.

People ought to get out of the international markets, unless something changes radically soon. I published a *Risk Report* in late 1993 in which I said what was really going on in the international markets. Foreign stocks and markets are overinflated. U.S. investors are chasing them higher, and most foreign markets are starting to reach all-time highs in an environment in which many smaller markets don't have much liquidity. For example, the entire Mexican economy is controlled by 36 families, and 20 of them determine what happens in the stock market.

Most investors, pros and amateurs, don't understand the language of countries where they're investing. These companies don't have to follow American accounting rules. The money flowing overseas is mostly a means to an end for countries receiving it, but that doesn't mean it's good for the investor. The investor who wants to participate in international moves should invest in companies that have a large international exposure or in countries that are listed on U.S. stock exchanges, subscribe to U.S. accounting standards, and have to comply with U.S. regulations.

## WHAT I LEARNED
◆

When I began writing this book, I was puzzled about what made a country economically successful. Like many others, I believed in the efficacy of private-public partnership—the idea that business creates progress and the government protects us from too much progress too fast, implemented too cruelly by big business.

But as I talked to my insiders and asked many questions about how our economy and economies overseas work, I began to detect a pattern in the answers. More and more insiders, including economists Murray Rothbard and Mark Skousen, convinced me of the truth of high savings rates—so long as these rates are translated into capital for investment—and low, steady interest rates (which ensures that business can plan for the future and invest in a rational way). *Rolling Stone* writer and Fed watcher William Grieder has pointed out that low-inflation economies can be construed as being unfair to small debtors and farmers, but on the whole, a low-inflation environment is certainly preferable to a high-inflation one—and economic progress is often secondarily about fairness and primarily about investment and construction.

Hardheaded country watcher Karl Zinsmeister knows that when you scratch the surface of such booming economies as those in Asia, you invariably find these underlying economic principles at work. And economists like Skousen probably have it right when they maintain that only investors who understand the truth about economic principles (who have internalized the idea that the government cannot manage the economy except possibly by setting up an environment in which low, or lower, interest rates and high savings rates flourish) are prepared to make intelligent decisions about foreign investing.

That a country conforms to a healthy economic profile doesn't mean an investment in any particular instrument in that country will simply accrue in value. That kind of approach would be naive indeed. Nonetheless, as Skousen explains, an investor who understands what makes an economy tick, understands why inflation comes about, and comprehends the steps that can be taken to build a healthy economy, is far more likely to be a successful international investor than one who doesn't understand such fundamentals. Additionally, the investor who understands the truth about the relationship between government and private enterprise and the results the fiat-money system must inevitably produce will be better prepared to invest domestically as well as overseas.

A 1993 *Economist* article stated that 96 percent of U.S. assets were still invested domestically. In the era of marketshock, a wise investor is likely to look elsewhere for growth. While such investors may, with more or less ease, discern promise in certain countries, they are likely to find it difficult to act on their convictions. As a result, they may want to use professional funds to direct their investing. Professional funds have a downside in that they are often run by insiders who have more of a stake in the financial industry than in garnering top-level results. But used judiciously, funds may add to an investor's portfolio and represent a way of garnering returns that the investor could not conveniently obtain without becoming a professional investor.

Of course, investment even in the most rapidly expanding economy will not be without ups and downs. A conversation with market watcher Richard Schmidt will cure anyone of the perception that global investing is safe or easy. Lack of liquidity, tax laws, unscrupulous government and private manipulation of markets, misleading accounting, all of these factors make international investing a tough haul over the long course. Wealth is not accumulated without risk.

# INVESTMENT SUMMARY
◆

## INTERNATIONAL INVESTING: DEFINITION OF THE PROBLEM

◆ International investing will be increasingly necessary as the world's equity capitalization expands relative to single-region capitalization, even taking into account continued political instability. This is especially true in the United States, where the market cap is expected to undergo massive shrinkage relative to the rest of the world. In this country and around the world, even as international trading explodes, most investors are still locked into local marketplaces.

◆ International investing is difficult for the average investor because of language difficulties, information difficulties, and lack of access to promising markets.

♦ International investing is confusing because most people lack certainty of what constitutes a successful economic environment. Country choice may be the most important choice of all when it comes to international investing, but even countries investors think they know can prove surprising. Japan's economic collapse, Italy's political upheavals, and the former Soviet Union's worsening difficulties took even experienced international observers by surprise.

## WHAT THE INVESTOR CAN DO

♦ Understand what constitutes a successful economic environment. Investors who wish to invest by themselves, in country funds or even in mutual funds, should try to educate themselves about country conditions worldwide to make the best choice of professional vehicles in which to place their assets.

♦ Figure out whether a targeted country or region is reflating or deflating. Investors must keep in mind that a repressive social agenda may not have any immediate impact on the economic vitality of the region.

♦ Pay careful attention to countries that have less in the way of government money power and punishing tax policies. Central banking interference in economic cycles should be a red flag to proceed with caution. Countries with the least federal banking interference—according to market observers like Skousen—are Switzerland, Hong Kong, and Singapore.

# CHAPTER THREE

# BIG MONEY

◆

## Value-Oriented,
## Single-Asset Strategies

Once an investor understands modern marketshock and comprehends the basics of real-life economics, he or she is ready to examine various investment alternatives. This chapter examines traditional Big Money investing around the world.

Big Money funds are large pools of private and public money run by Registered Investment Advisers (RIAs) who are licensed by the Securities and Exchange Commission (SEC). RIAs run private funds that are oftentimes bundled by Wall Street firms to form so-called wrap programs. These programs offer investors a choice of different money managers depending on the amount of risk the investor is willing to undertake and the strategy the investor seeks. Brokers who offer Wall Street wrap programs charge quarterly or annual fees ("wraps") and in return supposedly give the investor access to the busy money manager of his choice.

Wraps can also be built from mutual funds. And many RIAs start out as private money runners and then graduate to running mutual funds as well. In such cases, these money pros will often manage private and pension plan money in much the same way as they do their other pools of capital—following Employee Retirement Income Security Act (ERISA) rules and single-asset investment strategies for both portions.

Big Money is the most common kind of investment vehicle open to the average person, and therefore interviews with Big Money managers—mutual to begin with, then private at the end of the chapter—are an appropriate way to begin to examine internationally diversified investing. Big Money managers, international style, are neither so unpredictable nor secretive as New Money managers, whom we examine in the next part. Regulations like those found in ERISA and the 1944 Investment Act tend to restrict what these managers can do with public and plan funds.

Big Money investing overseas is a relatively new phenomenon; the bulk of overseas investing took place in the 1980s and has increased only gradually since then. Most Big Money overseas is still value-based; that is, the managers tend to scout around in various countries for stocks they consider to be underpriced relative to the market in that country. There are few Big Money managers, either private- or public-fund managers, who specialize in worldwide real estate or metals or currencies. Mostly, Big Money follows the line laid out for it in this country since the 1940s: It seeks undervalued stock or bond investments.

The problems associated with Big Money investing in the age of marketshock are many. For one thing, Big Money is often at the mercy of dealing firms who transact most of the trades Big Money wants to make. This means that firms in this country and around the world are intimately aware of the disposition of Big Money's portfolio and can run against it for a profit. This is apparently what happened during the crash of 1987, and there is no reason why it can't happen again unless electronic trading systems are put into place—along with the proper sureties—that allow Big Money managers to trade with each other over electronic nets. Unfortunately, the opposite is occurring; electronic international nets are being set up by dealers rather than by buyers and sellers. Globex, the international electronic futures exchange, is one example of a net that has been set up to exclude customers.

There is also the problem of single-instrument investing in general. A truly hedged Big Money fund would be invested in numerous instruments—the idea being that if one market moved one way, another market might move in the opposite direction. Such hedged investing currently runs into problems because of lack of liquidity. But as more electronic nets are established and linked (despite regulatory and securities industry foot-dragging), these liquidity issues may be, at least in part, resolved.

Computerization has certainly changed the way Big Money managers digest data and invest on their hunches and conclusions. And there are many on the buy side who would like to do more than they currently can. Numerous Big Money and New Money managers I spoke to expressed irritation with the way current regulations interact with the information age. Lack of leverage, prohibitions on short selling and cross-selling between markets and asset classes were constraints once looked on by regulators and the public as safety measures. But today, even granted sell-side rigidity, a thorough discussion of the kinds of new financial tools that Big Money finds useful would probably benefit professional and individual investors alike.

## OVERVIEW

### *"Funds should offer choices as sophisticated as the market is."*

REGINALD GREEN *runs a California-based mutual fund marketing service covering both Big Money and New Money funds.*

Certainly a mutual fund is the only way to go for the average investor. That's true domestically and even truer when investing abroad. Different accounting standards and currency changes make it a nightmare for the ordinary person to cope with. People who have invested in the U.S. stock market feel they're playing against the house, and that's even more true when investing internationally. An investor who has a portfolio manager may feel as if the odds are evened out. Obviously there's no guarantee that he or she will make the right decision.

There are several ways to look at the divergent strategies for investment among money managers. I make the distinction between subjective evaluation and quantitative strategies. By subjective evaluation I mean that these money managers do some number-crunching, but they also go out and meet the people managing the company—see whether they pay their bills on time, what their management strategy is. I see room for growth for both in that kind of investing and for the more quantitative school. Quantitative investing tends to bring out relationships that might not be available to the pure value investors. For instance, a quantitative manager recently told me that in Texas, banks tend to move in the same economic cycle as oil companies. Someone who is not doing that analysis and is invested in Texas in both banks and oil may think he is diversified but is not.

Especially with new instruments and new ways of investing, we need to have maximum disclosure in down-to-earth language. But there's no reason for some of the rules applying to the big public funds. There is no reason why people shouldn't have the opportunity to buy shares on margin. They should be able to make those kinds of choices. The funds should offer choices that are as sophisticated as the market is.

———————◆———————

## VALUE INVESTING

*"We're looking for promising industries and for companies that are well-run."*

DAVID BECKWITH *supervises two global equity mutual funds for one of the largest mutual fund and insurance groups, John Hancock.*

For both funds I run, the basic strategy is fundamental growth-stock investing. We're looking for promising industries and for companies that are well-run and well-established, with promising earnings growth. We also take possible currency fluctuations into account when we invest. We can do this by investing more or less in countries and stocks where we expect adverse currency fluctuations in the near or long term.

Currency is only one of the three Cs we worry about. The biggest C is the company itself. We are always engaged in country assessments, but if we like a stock, we're not going to say we're not going to invest in it just because we don't think the country is the greatest. A good company is a good company no matter where it is. If a company is a leader, it'll do well. We don't invest in indexes. The biggest thing for us to figure out is if we like the management. If management is not committed to the shareholder, we're going to be wary. We want to find out about them—how well established in the industry is the company, how strong are they, whether they are going to have to come to the market to grow or have other ways of raising capital. Other fundamentals include brand awareness—does the company have a widely known product— the company's overall position within the industry, and its market share outlook.

We're growth-oriented. We tend to gravitate to countries with strong overall growth and then look for companies with records of either previous growth or growth potential. In international investing there's always an accounting problem, and we'll probably never see parity between U.S. and overseas accounting methods. But we can use certain basic rules of thumb. For one thing, sales are sales. If a company's sales are growing, that's probably the least tainted number. There will always be swings, and the technology will always be there. Good money managers are able to block out the short term.

**BOB HEISTERBERG** *is a top-performing global analyst with Alliance Capital. He runs separate international accounts for pension plans of corporations.*

Alliance's historical claim to fame was U.S. equity management, whereby plan sponsors would hire a stable group of managers for domestic investing. Now we're getting more and more mandates abroad. The objective is to manage global equity.

At Alliance we could see the way the industry was changing—expanding and consolidating at the same time. We started broadening our mix, and now we're known for everything—equity, fixed income, currencies. But the markets have changed as fast as we have. The new derivative instruments have added volatility to the market. I always worried with futures and derivatives because these are on the periphery of the system, where you can't see the order flow. But someday the volume could swamp the central market just as portfolio insurance trading did during the crash of 1987.

Everything is an action and reaction, and I hope the regulators will be more thoughtful. The industry too has to think broadly about the possible consequences of new developments. Certainly progress is being made around the world in terms of new markets, with the liberalization and opening up in India, Korea, Latin America, Singapore, and Thailand. I expect these movements toward openness and markets for goods and services to continue. There's an old adage that trade is like a bicycle: You have to keep moving forward, or you fall over.

————————◆————————

## INTEGRATED APPROACH

*"Stock selection is less important than country selection."*

ALAN ALBERT *runs London-based Merrill Lynch Eurofund, managing both mutual fund and institutional money. A 30-year veteran of the international money scene, Albert is well-aware of the increasingly complex Big Money trends of modern global finance.*

I was trained, as were most others in the United Kingdom, with certain disciplines. The entry of American pension funds into the international investing scene and the questions they started asking made us think more deeply.

In the U.K., pension funds asked about return, average return and so on but not how that return was achieved. When America started investing overseas, managers asked what were the contributions to that return—stock selection, country selection and all the rest.

In Europe the investment mandate on the pension side of the scale was to let the professionals handle it and not ask too many questions. Now, how to get returns has became a factor. Our methodology is top-down, but it's an integrated approach that includes sector selection and stock selection using uniform factors. The same factors that make us pick a certain country are used for sector and stock selection as well.

Most large organizations work on the method of having an asset allocator decide on a top-down approach. He might want to put money in Japan because the yen seems to be appreciating, and that may mean bigger profits for Japanese companies. But if we decide to go to Japan because of a rising yen, we may avoid stocks specifically affected by the yen. If the yen is appreciating, then an investor should stay away from any export-related stock because exports will be adversely affected by a strengthening yen. If he wants to enter Japan because of a strong yen and take a position in an export-related company, he is actually working at cross-purposes. This problem of working at cross-purposes is more common than you might think. We get around it by having a very small team and we integrate our strategies. We should have 10 or 11 managers for the sort of money we're running, but we have fewer to keep the operation small and simple.

Recent analysis in the United States tended to show that stock selection was far less important than country selection. The researchers chose the 100 largest overseas managers and then broke down their investing patterns over a five- to eight-year period by country, currency stock selection. The conclusion is that virtually all the earnings came from country and currency selection—stock selection had zero value. That would seem to mean that people who believe they're stock selectors don't actually work that way or derive their profits from what they think they do.

We all have our favorite stocks, but between the failures and successes it can be a zero-sum game. A lot does depend on the time scale of the analysis and selection. In a normal stock cycle, we think that in at least three of those five years, country selection is more important, and in any two years the stock might be the more important. In a recovery cycle, the stock becomes more important. But you come back to the basic contention that more value comes from the country, though we believe we can add value through stock selection. I would like to be able to use other investment tools as well. I think derivatives are going to be increasingly commonplace parts of institutional and even individual portfolios.

ANTHONY REGAN *runs the $1 billion high-performance Putnam Global Growth Fund. Additionally, Regan manages about $800 mil-*

*lion in pension plans and over the past five years has ranked in the top
5 percent in his performance with those plans.*

We are active managers. We use our judgment based on a strong
and consistent growth. We believe that picking the right countries and the right stocks is important. We try to add value in
both areas.

When we pick countries, we have a universe of 27 that we
choose from. Our objective is to identify the most attractive 10
and get most of the portfolio invested in those 10. Seven out of
10 is all right. Occasionally we'll get a higher score. We try to
get countries and stocks right, and the analysis shows that both
areas have contributed. We compare the prices we pay for companies' assets, the book value, and price-to-book compared with
the profitability of the company—the measure we take there is
return on equity. We compare those figures and can see when
the two numbers are out of line in terms of their relationship to
the market. Then our real work is to go back in time and do a
lot of number-crunching to reveal trends to see if the numbers
are trustworthy. Then we visit the company.

Particularly in the past two years, as most of the world has
been in recession, our process and approach has led us into mostly
defensive stocks. I'm thinking of stocks like food manufacturing
and pharmaceuticals.

What's ahead? Our policy is based on interest rates coming
down a long way, leading to some recovery in 1994. What that
will mean is that we can start to see corporate-profits growth in
many of our countries of 15 to 20 percent—certainly in the
interest-rate-sensitive stocks like the financial area and also in
construction-related and consumer spending stocks. For 1995 the
hope is that we'll get sustained recovery—not spectacular but
steady rates of growth with low inflation and therefore low interest
rates.

◆

## INDEXING

### *"Some of our competitors have been hesitant to offer passively managed funds."*

GUS SAUTER *supervises $16 billion in international and domestic funds for the gigantic mutual fund organization the Vanguard Group. He also oversees the firm's quantitative research efforts.*

Vanguard offers a number of stock and bond index funds that track both domestic and international indexes. In fact, Vanguard is the leader of mutual fund indexing for individual investors, offering 16 portfolios.

Vanguard's leadership in index funds relates to our "at cost" structure. Vanguard is unique in that the mutual funds jointly own the corporation. Some of our competitors have been hesitant to offer passively managed funds because such portfolios have minuscule expense ratios that offer fund sponsors little profit.

We have a lineup of three equity index portfolios: a European fund, a Pacific fund, and a new emerging-markets fund. In addition to our index funds, which are managed in-house, we offer investors a whole line of traditionally managed stock and bond funds.

Indexing is a modern investment strategy made possible in large part by the power of the computer. Now enhanced indexing is becoming popular. You can enhance returns by tracking an index and then weighting it with stocks you think are going to perform especially well. The goal is to outperform the index on a consistent basis. We believe that enhanced indexing is a growing segment of active management.

Vanguard offers international index vehicles. International investing makes sense, not so much for the potential for higher return but for diversification. Historically, stock markets around the world haven't all moved in exactly the same way at the same time, and by investing a certain amount of money overseas an investor can smooth out volatility. The U.S. equity market decline during the first quarter of 1994 could signal the end of a long bull run. At the same time, markets around the world are at different stages of recovery, so it makes sense to diversify internationally. Typically, a particular market will achieve its best results when the corresponding economy is just starting to come out of a recession.

---

◆

---

## ENHANCED INDEXING

### *"We try to beat the index."*

HARU SAWADA *manages Asian investments for Nomura's $5 billion capital management, affiliated with the hugely powerful Japanese brokerage, Nomura.*

We manage on a global basis, investing over $30 billion in equity and fixed income, with investments from institutions around the world. We run mutual funds too. We have four offices—one each in Tokyo, London, New York, and Singapore, with Tokyo being the headquarters. Each organization has regional client responsibility and regional investment responsibility. The fund I manage, the Pacific Basin Fund, has as its objective long-term capital gains. We're a no-load fund, so we do business with some of the smaller pension plans that prefer to buy this kind of fund rather than tapping a separate manager.

We try to beat the index—mainly the Morgan Stanley Capital International Pacific Basin Index, which includes Japan, Hong Kong, Australia, New Zealand, Singapore, and Malaysia. Korea is opening up as a market too, though before 1992 foreigners couldn't invest much. The Philippines and Thailand are small markets. We're trying to find undervalued stocks to hold for at least two to three years. We use research reports from Nomura Research Institute and from its partners. They give us personal support as well. Also our portfolio managers in various regions visit the companies in which we're investing, or want to invest, to try to find out if they are fairly valued in terms of assets and cash flow. You have to compare the prospects of the company to its competitors, compare them to the same industry and to the markets. There are four or five different factors to look at.

Our money management style is quite conservative. We think it is hard to add value through plain vanilla index investing. Rather, we use index investments for risk reduction and diversification purposes. We'll also underweight or overweight, diverging from the index if we think it's warranted. The degree of divergence from the index is not large. We have limitations of 30 percent for a big country where we're comfortable—less in a small one.

Since we're investing long-term, currency risk becomes a secondary concern. If we are strongly confident that a certain currency is overvalued and we're investing there, we may hedge, but it's rare for us to do that. We'd rather hedge through stock exposure than currency. That means if we think currency is moving down in a particular country against another currency, we'll look for a company that does a good deal of business in that other currency. If the currency moves the way we expect, the company takes its profits and its stock reflects the move. Long term, we believe that we'll get results. That's the picture we use.

———————◆———————

## CURRENCY HEDGES

*"We'll hedge with forwards or options—whatever instrument is more attractive."*

DAVE MANNHEIM *is in charge of a worldwide equity funds for Massachusetts-based MFS.*

Our funds have various investment objectives, and our capital appreciation fund is invested everywhere, in both the United States and abroad, with a bias toward growth and leaders in the industry. Our approach is bottom-up. We're stock pickers. We make decisions on a stock-by-stock basis, by focusing on company fundamentals. Right now we're 50 percent in Europe, 30 percent in North America, and 20 percent in Japan and elsewhere in Asia-Pacific, including Malaysia, Korea, and Hong Kong.

In Mexico, where we try to maintain an investment presence, my favorite stock is Grupo Televisa, a company active in all aspects of media and entertainment. In Hong Kong we like Dairy Farm, a food retailer operating around the world—in Australia, New Zealand, Singapore, and Spain. In Japan there aren't currently very many attractive companies—maybe Sega, the video-game firm. In Korea we've invested in Hansol, a paper company. In Sweden we like Astra, the pharmaceutical company, and Svenska Handelsbanken, the only remaining nongovernment-supported bank.

We take country risk into account in that we won't put a large percentage of our investments in any one country. Insofar as currencies are concerned, we make the stock call first and then make a separate call as to currency risk. We hedge currencies not to make a profit but to reduce risk. We'll hedge with forwards or options—whatever instrument is more attractive. Our rule of thumb is to hedge if there's a possibility of a 10 percent or more move in the currency—if we think the dollar would strengthen that amount or more in the country where we're invested. Currency hedging is a zero-sum game. Sometimes you win, and sometimes you lose. We think you make the money in the stocks.

The place you can't hedge is in the emerging markets like Brazil because there aren't currency markets for those countries. If we can't hedge, then we make a pure stock bet. We try to look at the firm's dollar earnings to see if the investment is good enough to offset the currency risk.

We've been outside the United States since 1986 and have seen a lot of changes. Today, everything is becoming globalized, including companies. Nestlé is based in Switzerland, but it might derive 90 percent or more of its profits overseas.

———————◆———————

## FIXED INCOME

### *"Europe has a way to go."*

GARY KREPS *is fixed-income director of top-performing GT Global international funds.*

Bonds thrive on bad news. When economies go sour, central bankers tend to lower interest rates to stimulate growth. As interest rates move down, bond prices move up. Germany is Europe's engine, but it's been slowed by the acquisition of East Germany, and German bankers will have to lower rates to stimulate the economy. When that happens, rates will move down across the entire yield curve, not only in Germany but in the rest of Europe as well, and the trend will certainly hold through 1994.

There's no mystery about what's going on in Europe. One of

the keys to understanding economic activity is to watch the central bankers. You can go back to the crash of 1987 and see a pattern that continues today. Europe has a way to go before its linked economies turn around. There are definite opportunities, especially in the peripheral European countries of Spain, Italy, and Denmark. In developing countries that are trying to get their economy in shape by squeezing interest rates to counteract inflationary pressures, there's also opportunity. Countries like Poland, Morocco, and Argentina are either driving rates down or holding them in a low range, creating buying opportunities or at least a good environment in which to hold fixed-income instruments.

LES NANBERG *runs MFS's huge international fixed-income investments, some $3.5 billion in non-U.S. instruments. All told, MFS has about $34 billion in assets, with about 70 percent in fixed income.*

There are not many tax-exempt instruments overseas like the municipal bond market here, but there are plenty of government instruments: German bunds, English gilts, Japanese government bonds.

The focus of our process is to make specific decisions as to what markets are the most attractive. We're top-down investors, in that we look at the world in economic blocks and try to ascertain what's promising and where we can freely trade, such as Japan. We're especially active in the dollar block, which consists of the United States, Canada, Australia, and New Zealand. We also are extremely active in the European and Japanese blocks.

We have two different types of pools at MFS for bonds. Our global bond fund focus is total return, so we're not so geared to a high level of current income. One of our other pools is geared to yield. That's invested one-third in domestic Treasurys, one-third in junk, and one-third in foreign instruments.

The currency direction is a major part of the investment process. We're always asking what kind of environment the U.S. dollar is going to give us. We do see a strong dollar environment. The economy seems to be recovering, and to the extent that continues, the recovery is beneficial to the dollar.

———————◆———————

## EQUITY TREND FOLLOWING

### *"Americans who want to invest abroad are forcing a revolution."*

PAUL ROGGE *manages AIM's successful domestic and international mutual funds. AIM's quantitative methods and trend-tracking strategies are akin to strategies used by some futures traders.*

AIM has had a lot of success with its two domestic funds, especially its flagship domestic fund. AIM International Equity uses the same philosophy that has been used at AIM since the 1960s. Instead of trying to sit in Houston where we're headquartered and take a position and try to fight the markets, we try to work with the market. When we see significant earnings, we jump in if we're comfortable. We make decisions based on consensus earnings expectations and use electronic stock-research services. We also talk to about 30 brokers internationally on a regular basis about where earnings in industries and companies are going.

When you first hear about a system like this, you'd think there would be a lot of turnover. But the way we judge stocks, if we're right, one positive surprise leads to another, so we can ride a trend for a long time. We are quick and news oriented, and we think our kind of investing is aided by technology and also by countries opening up their markets to investors. By using electronic services, we become more efficient in using local knowledge, which does save on resources. U.S. investors have kept most of their assets at home, but as more and more stocks are listed on exchanges outside the United States, opportunities to move outside increase as well. Americans who want to invest abroad are forcing revolution in financial services and changing the industry for the better.

————————◆————————

FUND INFORMATION

*"The most important thing for investors to know is what they're getting."*

AMY ARNOTT *is an analyst for the highly successful mutual fund information and tracking group Morningstar Mutual Funds.*

We cover funds with all kinds of different investment objectives. Our foreign stock group invests exclusively overseas. Funds in world stock could have a significant portion of their exposure in the United States. We also cover world bond funds and the short-term world income funds.

Funds tend to have specialized objectives. From a portfolio management standpoint it makes sense to rely on a division of labor. Another reason is the thinking that managers should let investors make their own asset allocation decisions. Funds are becoming more and more narrowly defined because by defining themselves narrowly people have a better chance of being a leader in a given sector. But there's also a blurring of international and domestic investing.

We've been trying to provide many different tools for investors to use, such as the percentage in foreign stocks for domestic funds. It can be useful to split up managers conceptually by their strategies, but it's also important to look at the payoff—not only the strategy but how they implement it. You could have two managers who have different ways of operating but end up with the same portfolio.

Everyone I've talked to sees slow growth around the world with no problems from inflation. But I suppose there could be a prolonged bear market. In that case, I think some of the oil funds—specialized sector funds that invest in energy and natural resources—would provide a hedge.

There are probably around 4,000 mutual funds all told. The most important thing for investors is to know what they're getting. Even with so many funds, investors are not automatically diversified by buying some. They have to diversify on their own.

———————◆———————

## SLOW GROWTH

### *"Investors will turn to growth stocks for a pop."*

EDGAR LARSEN *is senior portfolio manager for Transamerica Fund Management, where he runs an emerging growth fund.*

If we agree that we're not going to see a high-growth environment in this country over the next few years, then it makes sense to invest in growth stocks. These small companies can grow more than three times as fast as the Standard and Poor's (S&P) stocks, and we think we can be right about which ones to invest in about 60 percent of the time. We try to buy and hold, but if we realize things aren't working, we take our medicine and get out.

Prudent investors who understand business cycles and realize the kind of business conditions we're facing over the next few years should certainly consider growth stocks as part of their portfolios. In our Emerging Growth Fund, our target companies all have caps below $1 billion. We're looking all around the country for these promising small companies, and around the world as well. We tend to be rifle-shot buyers of international equity. But we're interested in South America, for instance, after the North American Free Trade Agreement (NAFTA) takes hold.

Investors should understand that in a slow-growth, inflationary environment, there's not much that can yield an outstanding return. Real estate won't appreciate, and bonds won't be offering high yields. Large stocks will tend to be sluggish. That's when investors will turn to growth stocks for a pop.

---◆---

## WRAP FEES AND NEW STRATEGIES

*"What investors aren't going to get from funds is true diversification."*

LARRY CHAMBERS *is a former top E.F. Hutton broker and the author of several books on investing, including one on wrap fees.*

Big Money diversification means mostly stock and bond diversification. Most money managers, even private money managers, diversify in stocks and bonds but not much else. Wrap fee investing programs are offered by Wall Street firms, but Wall Street has turned the wrap fee service into a product that is more hype than a diversified investing system.

A Wall Street firm will offer a wrap fee program to a customer, in which the customer will pay a certain amount to gain access to funds managed by top private money managers. The customer will pay the firm a set amount to manage the money for a year and may then gain access to these money managers. The problem is that the manager will probably manage only one asset class— stocks, bonds, what have you. The customer who wants to be thoroughly diversified must think about investing in different kinds of assets around the country and even around the world.

There are other more well-known problems involved with wrap fee programs—the fee itself, for instance, though that may be coming down.

But no load or load, wrap fee or no wrap fee, what investors aren't going to get from funds is true diversification across asset classes and strategies. You might get a little bit of it, but you'd have to work very hard to achieve it.

Instead, especially at the top of the cycle, some mutual funds try to entice investors by boosting yield through risky kinds of investment strategies. This wouldn't be quite so bad if the fund had the wherewithal to hedge risks with other asset classes.

By seeking yield, an investor can end up with too little yield for too much risk.

———————◆———————

## PRIVATE FUNDS

### *"Most managers tend to be stock- and bond-oriented."*

DAN BOTT *is a top broker and consultant with Smith Barney, running some $500 million. He's also a pioneer of new-style brokerage, which involves consulting and asset management through funds and private money managers.*

Most money managers in this country are dealing with domestic securities. If they do deal with foreign securities, most of them would be in American depository receipts investing in big over-seas companies like Royal Dutch Shell and Nestlé.

The difference between a mutual fund and a money manager is that the money manager can go ahead and respond to specific restrictions and customize the account the way the investor wants it. He can invest individually and not pool an investor's cash with others', the way mutual funds do.

Most people don't understand the difference between a privately managed fund and a mutual fund. A private fund manager is registered with the SEC as a registered investment adviser. The SEC registration gives the manager the authority to invest in stocks and bonds. If commodity trading is involved, the manager has to be licensed by the Commodities Futures Trading Commission.

On the whole, money management has tended to be conservative. Money managers in this country tend to be mostly stock- and bond-oriented. Real estate, for instance, is hard for a money manager to get in and out of. Most managers, especially those for individual money, have been afraid to use technology stocks, and they've been succumbing to investors' fears of investing overseas.

In this sector, international management overseas comes from the private managers' running institutional money. About 80 percent of all professional money management has to do with pension plan money. But the U.S. market has grown to six times the size it was in the early 1970s, while the world's capitalization has grown some 20 times. Private managers are venturing overseas just as mutual funds and hedge funds are.

WILLIAM SPETRINO *is managing director of client services for ICC Gratry Global, a division of the registered investment adviser, Orlando, Florida-based Investment Counsel Company. ICC runs some $700 million nationally and worldwide.*

ICC Gratry Global is a relatively new division that gives the pension plans and wealthy clients ICC serves the chance to invest internationally through ICC. ERISA funds and high-net-worth individuals are comfortable with registered investment advisers.

Most fund managers want to see that registration at both state and federal levels.

Most global money managers have two basic decisions to make: Are they going to pursue a top-down or bottom-up investment strategy? Are they going to invest in core or emerging markets?

At ICC Gratry, we allocate money using a top-down approach. First, we use a macroanalysis that allows us to get a good economic reading for the country and its political and economic trends. Then we'll focus on the state of the market, and finally on certain stocks.

We're a core manager. We want to invest in markets that are large enough to be liquid. That's why we invest in such major markets as Germany, France, Sweden, Switzerland, Japan, Hong Kong, Australia, Canada, and Mexico.

International money management is still in its developmental stage here in the United States. We're puzzled as to what's taking so long. Gratry & Company has been managing global assets since 1981.


MICHAEL O'HARA *is a top portfolio manager for Murray Johnstone International, a well-known Scottish money manager running $8 billion in private and pension money and through Wall Street wrap programs.*

We're a Scottish firm based in Glasgow, and our focus is primarily international. We have about $8 billion under management for private clients and pension plans such as Hallmark Cards. We're also involved in wrap fee programs with such firms as Smith Barney.

Our 60 investment professionals take a top-down approach. Country allocations are the first step. We're seeking the right exposure in the right market at the right time. We would classify ourselves as market timers.

Once we've gone top-down and chosen the country and exposure, then we'll begin to go bottom-up, spending 12 to 20 weeks traveling in the country every year, kicking the tires. It's very difficult to get a sound understanding of a company overseas unless you go out and speak to them and see the plants. International investing is growing. The data are available more quickly now, and the figures are more reliable.

Overseas, especially in Europe, there has always been an awareness of international investing, more cross-pollination between countries. But recently the U.S. mutual funds have been aggressive about setting up overseas efforts, though the average U.S. private money manager, the registered investment adviser, has been a little slower to react.

It takes a lot of money to do serious overseas investing—it's a big undertaking—especially bottom-up value investing where the manager is trying to get a sense of individual companies. There have to be people on the ground. A manager might have to be running better than $2 billion a year before thinking about mounting an international effort like that.

# WHAT I LEARNED

Fund watchers Larry Chambers and Dan Bott helped open my eyes to some of the basic issues involved with Big Money investing. They reminded me of Big Money's historical pedigree, which harkens back to bank trust departments. Big Money's single-instrument emphasis, lengthy time horizons, and unhedged positions stem from the conservative, and some would say simplistic, strategies pursued by bank investment counselors throughout the 19th and 20th centuries.

Ironically, as Chambers points out, this same conservative approach to investment in the marketshock era can lead to increased risk-taking. The very nature of single-instrument investing—the kind favored by Big Money for mostly regulatory reasons—is the kind that some would say is ultimately the most dangerous, at least in the hands of some managers at some funds. Of course, as Big Money keeps getting bigger, the same kind of investor abuses that occur on Wall Street will begin to be a more common Big Money problem: front-running, fund-rigging, data and performance juggling. For Big Money, as for Wall Street, the problem remains one of industry-regulatory gridlock. Big Money's confusing fee structures, for instance, stem in part from the regulatory mandate against performance fees under which mutual funds operate. Managers who run futures funds can take performance fees upwards of 15 percent and 20 percent and often do, but mutual fund regs prohibit such performance fees. This form of primitive price-fixing has led, as the industry expands, to a proliferation of "load" and "no-load" sales charge structures, all of them conforming to specific regulatory guidelines.

As a result, customers have been further confused. The so-called no-load fund industry has convinced consumers that by buying a fund with no up-front fee, the consumer is saving money. But in place of an up-front fee, which is really a commission paid to a fund salesman (a wirehouse rep or independent broker), the no-load fund may be spending a good deal of money on advertising. Additionally, the no-load fund may resort to considerably more risky investments to boost yield because, lacking a sales force, it needs to attract attention to itself to boost its marketing effort. This is not to say that load funds are better or worse than no-load funds, only that in an environment where load and no-load products compete on an absolutely level playing field because of similar regulations, only those who are economically illiterate will think one product has an innate advantage over the other. Taken as a group, what no-load funds offer the consumer in up-front savings they may withdraw in advertising charges and the increased risk of their strategies.

Still, Big Money offers average investors some positives—most important, an opportunity to diversify internationally through both indexing and value investing, especially in stock markets. Listening to fund marketer Reg Green and top manager David Beckwith, I began to understand how Big Money, with its single-country funds, regional funds, and worldwide investment strategies, facilitates investment in specific areas of the globe, allowing investors to pinpoint those parts of the world where they see the most promising low-rate and high-savings environment. What Big Money doesn't do, within individual funds, is give investors the kind of asset allocation and strategy diversification that are called for in the age of marketshock.

Unfortunately, as some of my insiders never fail to point out, domestic Big Money continues to trade in large measure through Wall Street. So long as this situation continues, Big Money will continue its incestuous relationship with the dealer community. And dealers, in turn, will continue to use Big Money, from time to time, as trading fodder fueling different and more profitable positions—often at investors' expense.

# INVESTMENT SUMMARY

## Big Money: Difficulties of Diversifying

♦ Diversification is a necessary part of a modern investor's portfolio, but there are still relatively few ways investors can diversify internationally within a fund, especially a Big Money fund, beyond one or two instruments. Investors can diversify by being invested in several funds, but this is not the same as being diversified within a single fund.

♦ Diversification is not easily achievable in a single country with a slowly growing market cap (the United States). Therefore, motivated domestic investors will look outside their own country to try to make use of the available vehicles.

♦ International diversification in equity or any other instrument is difficult for most investors to accomplish without professional help. Investors willing to pay for it can receive help from planners or brokers. The trick is to try to discern top professional investors with sympathetic styles, a difficult task unless the investor understands modern financial trends and the underlying economics of nations or regions in question.

## WHAT THE INVESTOR CAN DO

♦ Realize that true diversification is not likely to come about from an investment in a single Big Money fund, or even several such funds. To ensure maximum equity diversification within Big Money limitations, investors should seek funds with consistently good international track records, bearing in mind that past performance is no guarantee of future results.

♦ Make a distinction among various kinds of Big Money strategies to determine whether the kind of investing the Big Money runner is using is appropriate to the regional or country cycle. This means examining the strategies the Big Money manager is using, as well as asset classes in which the Big Money fund is invested.

♦ When using Big Money funds, be prepared to diversify across strategies and asset classes and then adopt a long-term outlook using macroallocation as a hedge. Big Money is not the kind of investment that ordinarily gives a quick killing.

## BIG MONEY PROBLEMS THAT REMAIN

♦ Big Money is inherently one-dimensional, using a variety
of strategies to invest mainly in single instruments (equity
or fixed income) around the world. Big Money's structural
rigidity lends itself to front-running (by Wall Street firms
and private money pros) and risky strategies to boost yield.
Big Money's lack of imaginative investment strategies is
aggravated by its fee structure. Lacking incentives, Big
Money's main revenue is derived from fees, a form of compensation that nearly guarantees mediocre results.

♦ Most U.S.-style Big Money can't sell short. Big Money is
ordinarily constrained by domestic rules from playing the
"downside" of the market, that is, making a bet that the
market will move down instead of up. Big Money can't use
leverage and needs to keep cash on hand for redemptions.
While certain New Money funds are beginning to use futures, the majority of Big Money funds—especially consumer funds—remain unhedged vehicles invested long.

♦ Big Money can't use leverage to the degree that other kinds
of investment vehicles (like Hot Money) can. Big Money
funds are, on the whole, constrained from using leverage,
in part because most still don't use futures but also because
any leverage that Big Money does embrace must be offset
by reserves—funds left in cash and therefore useless for
investment purposes.

CHAPTER FOUR

# NEW MONEY

◆

## Allocation, Timing, and Hedging

New Money is more adventurous than Big Money. The individual investor who has chosen among Big Money funds, taking into account economic climate, is now ready to examine New Money strategies. New Money may actually be less risky than Big Money, though given the constraints on mutual fund-style New Money and the continued existence of physical-exchange trading, this is an open question. The marketshock-savvy individual investor ought to subject New Money managers to careful scrutiny before investing. Even then, the investor ought to employ what retail sales pro Howard Silverman (see Chapter Six) calls an outlier strategy, placing only a modest portion of assets in the more risky New Money strategies.

What exactly is New Money? It comes in several forms, but its outstanding qualities are the utilization of different kinds of instruments worldwide, hedging strategies across various instruments, and, the most controversial of its characteristics, asset allocation and market timing in various guises.

Steve Shellans, editor of Portland, Oregon-based *MoniResearch* newsletter, follows market timers and has divided market timing strategies and practitioners into subcategories. Shellans, a pioneering reporter in this field, himself admits that the kinds of investing that the computer is giving rise to are so new that there are no names. "You can just make up your own," he says. Shellans defines market timing as moving an entire lump sum in and out of a single asset class, usually into cash. A money pro who moves an entire lump sum out of several assets is practicing tactical asset allocation. On the whole, it seems to me that market-timing has a more radical connotation than asset allocation— a discipline that implies reweighting assets rather than the wholesale removal of them from one asset class to another.

Unfortunately, many market timing, and even asset allocation strategies in these subcategories, use methods that are hard for the average investor to understand or believe in. Isolating historical stock patterns and trying to predict buying or selling points based on them is one popular but controversial method. Seasonality—buying or selling instruments, mostly equity, based on certain days, weeks, months or years—is another strategy that would surely strike some as unorthodox—not based on any deeper economic theory but rather on observations of data that may or may not be valid in the long term.

In aggregate, New Money may use some of these specific strategies. But an investor who believes in asset management, or even, occasionally, as the situation warrants, business-cycle timing, will find he actually has much in common with top New Money managers. These managers, often institutional in nature, seem well aware of the interaction of government regulation and private markets. They may have internalized business-cycle theory in practice, even if they haven't been exposed to the formal texts. They're aware that a fiat-money environment has made it more and more difficult for them to invest with any certainty of profit. They understand that a sudden marketshock, a combination of government action and computer power, can seriously damage their performance or even wipe them out.

Such managers aren't necessarily speculators, though often central bankers through certain portions of the business media would seek to characterize them that way. True, New Money managers will bet on the movements of certain international instruments. But the bet will often be linked to an understanding of macro-economic forces. Like currency traders, New Money managers may bet that a certain country's money is going to rise or fall depending on where in the business cycle that country's economy sits. They may bet that despite the best efforts of the country's central bankers to support the currency, it will ultimately fall relative to other countries' currencies because the country has just passed an onerous tax or is inflating to support generous social policies. Thus, what I call business-cycle asset allocation, the practice of weighting certain investments classes more heavily than others based on classical Austrian business theory, may well be a preferred method for a growing number of these new-style managers.

The simplest way to divvy up Big Money and New Money would have been to characterize Big Money as value-oriented investing and New Money as quantitative investing across instruments and asset classes with differing risk profiles. While I may agree that these strategies are among the most imaginative responses to a fiat-money environment, New Money is larger than any single strategy. In fact, in the future, investors may well take into account strategy and style as well as asset-class diversification. The investor, for instance, may not wish to take sides in the controversy between efficient market money pros who invest through indexes and those money pros who continue to make a living successfully picking out individual stocks. The investor may diversify among diversified funds, with arbitrage funds, with funds that perform intermarket hedging. As the computer breaks down securities segementation, more and more choices, strategies, and markets will be available to the individual investor.

New Money managers can perform arbitrages between different asset classes in different countries, can utilize market-timing strategies generated by artificial intelligence programs, and can develop sophisticated hedging and short-selling tactics around the world. It is the computer itself that makes the difference, breaking down regulatory structures, making available new data streams and allowing users to manipulate information to create and trade entirely new products.

New Money managers may be institutional-style managers practicing tactical asset allocation. Or they may be private money pros like Robert Gordon, who "sleeps with the tax code" and arbitrages between international equity markets, stripping dividends out of stock and reselling them for a profit in entirely new markets. The most intriguing and secretive group of equity-oriented fund managers run so-called hedge funds, which began springing up domestically in the 1950s, going long and selling short on the New York Stock Exchange (NYSE), hedging their clients' investments through use of this strategy.

Organized for wealthy individuals and offered through limited partnerships of 99 persons or fewer, hedge funds are the stuff of much envious Wall Street rumor and gossip. Like many of Wall Street's most successful instruments and strategies, hedge funds are constantly remaking themselves, and the lines between these funds and futures funds are starting to blur. One insider I spoke to maintained that the difference between a hedge fund and a futures fund was that a hedge fund held 15 percent or less of its money in derivatives. But as regulatory impediments lessen and information becomes increasingly available, the nomenclature becomes less important even as the profit—and risk—increases. To complicate the picture, a whole new wave of trading software is about to slosh over the global scene that has to do with new kinds of software just now starting to be used by traders: Artificial intelligence (AI).

Once considered an esoteric and highly limited way of analyzing vast amounts of complex data, AI—or the use of advanced software that is capable of being "trained" to "recognize" specific developments (such as price patterns and trading volume changes)—is now being viewed as a viable tool in the investment arsenal. As more and more corporations and day traders use this kind of technology, the market's velocity, especially (at least to begin with) the stock market's velocity, its interday trading movements, will increase dramatically.

It would be nice to wish away the effects of modern technology in the world's marketplaces, but the kinds of macromarket trading that computers allow will increase, not decrease, in the coming years. A fiat-money environment coupled with the huge capital flows inherent in the new kinds of investing coming down the pike signal increased volatility in the future.

New Money strategies are more or less risky depending on who is applying them. A savvy hedge-fund manager with deep pockets can mix and match various investment strategies and instruments not for regulatory reasons, but to make bets on a tricked-up—but profitable—global business cycle. Investors should be far more wary of rigid investment vehicles bound by regulations that are an impediment to true New Money diversification no matter how many bets on the underlying are made. Still, certain Big Money mutual funds are making attempts at using appropriate New Money strategies to add richness and diversification to their investing efforts (SoGen and Colonial— see upcoming section—are examples of innovative Big Money investing within a securitized environment).

What about private money runners? In this country, Registered Investment Advisers (RIAs) running private money are far less bound up by 20th century financial regulations than mutual funds. Yet because of their conservative, bank and trust-department past, private money managers are still more comfortable with individual instrument selecting (stock picking) than with New Money strategies. In this country, it is hedge funds and institutional Hot Money—futures funds—which have led the way toward international New Money investing.

As hedge funds become more international in nature and more venturesome in their choice of instruments, the dividing line between hedge funds and international futures funds will continue to blur. Given the increasing international scope and sophistication of Wall Street's top money runners, investors will be well advised to try to place at least some assets with such funds—if they have the means.

There is another compelling reason for hedge funds' success, and that has to do with information flow. Wall Street tends to use the order flow of Big Money and some New Money funds as trading fodder for its own positions. But as I pointed out in *Rebuilding Wall Street,* hedge funds, with their more sophisticated trading techniques and close relationships to Wall Street firms, often know what Wall Street knows. Despite their so-called buy-side origination, large hedge funds often act more like the sell side when it comes to getting information first about where markets are headed.

◆

## OVERVIEW

### *"We use technology to combine both value and growth strategies."*

**DANIEL RIE** *is director of equity investments for the prestigious mutual funds group of Colonial Investors.*

Our process is largely data driven. In our global fund we look for value within a given country and then select the country weights in a way that we think balances off the opportunities. We analyze the data of each country to find the favorable stocks and then use those in combination with the targets we have set. Our targets include what other global funds are doing; and our goal is to outperform those funds. In order to do that, we find it useful to use international databases that reflect the international analysts' opinion on various equity.

We use technology to combine both value and growth strategies. Pure value investors do better in a choppy market. Growth investors do better in a strong bull market. Our strategies allow us to switch from strategy to strategy.

Take AIM and Templeton. There you have different philosophies, and neither is going to change a lot. AIM is more quantitative and growth-oriented. Templeton is a value play. Both are fairly entrenched in a particular style of investing. One way for an investor to take advantage of those dissimilar styles is to switch back and forth, depending on what the market is doing. The investor could apply portfolio diversification to the managers' strategies as well as to investments.

Global diversification allows an investor to take some of the risk out of the portfolio. Someone who is invested in the United States, Europe, and Japan can get a lot of diversification in the portfolio, so overall volatility will be diminished. At the same time, the area where diversification can work most effectively is in emerging countries. Some of the rewards earned by investors in some of these countries have been exceptionally high. The risks are high too. The strategy is to build the right kind of portfolio that holds no more risk than the United States but includes developing countries and therefore holds a lot more in the way of rewards. The average investor should be invested 60 and 70 percent at home, 70 to 80 percent in developed countries, and 20 to 30 percent in developing countries. To me that's a very attractive combination.

———————◆———————

## COMMODITIES AND CURRENCY

*"We're looking at absolutely everything:*
*foreign equity, fixed income, real estate*
*investment trusts, gold-related securities."*

ELIZABETH TOBIN *is an analyst at the famous $1 billion maverick investment fund, SoGen, a U.S. mutual fund subsidiary of the French bank Société Générale. Unique among most mutual funds, SoGen's charter allows the fund to invest in many different instruments.*

We look for investment opportunities across various types of instruments. We're looking at absolutely everything: Foreign equities, fixed income, real estate investment trusts, gold-related securities—anything where we think we're buying something at a reasonable price. There are things we can't invest in—derivatives, futures, options, and commodities, for example.

Our job is to put investors in the right situation and to lower risk. We've done well. As of March 31, 1993, our one-year compounded annualized return is 14.8 percent, three-year is 11.4 percent, and 10-year is 14.9 percent—all without the load. On a risk-adjusted basis, according to Morningstar, our performance is in the top 10 percent.

We can do some currency hedging when we invest in foreign securities, although we normally do not hedge. We're mostly concerned with what we pay when we buy something—we were not willing to pay multiples required to participate in the Japanese markets. We won't pay 10 or 15 times cash flow for anything. We're value investors on an absolute basis. Something that looks cheap in an expensive environment may not be a good buy for us. Since our approach is a company-oriented one, we'll buy anywhere we find value. We're buying in Europe, Turkey,

Greece, and the Pacific Rim. We're more comfortable investing in established markets.

I don't expect there will be much difference between now and what we will be doing three years from now. We can hold for a long time. It's a unique approach that has worked. Why should we change? It's what we know.

———————◆———————

## CONTRARIAN STRATEGIES

*"Mutual funds have been created for the most part during this bull market, and that's one of the reasons I think so many of them invest only in stocks."*

RANDY HECHT *is president of San Francisco-based Robertson Stephens' Investment Trust and chief operating officer of Robertson Stephens & Co., an institutional brokerage firm that runs three mutual funds: contrarian, emerging growth, and value plus. Contrarian funds—a rare breed— invest against the common wisdom.*

This contrarian fund is one of only a few out like it and one of a very few to have the flexibility to invest anywhere in the world in any type of security that the portfolio manager sees fit to invest in. We have the opportunity to sell short and to invest in options and precious metals to help attain our goal of maximum capital growth.

Mutual funds have been created for the most part during this bull market, and that's one of the reasons I think so many of them invest only in stocks. If we see a bear market, we'll likely see many new funds that will invest in instruments besides stocks, but we haven't hit a real bear yet.

The early 1990s were a period of a stock boom, but the managers of this contrarian fund, going against the common wisdom, think there are a number of things that can derail the kinds of returns that investors are seeking. Rising interest rates, the U.S. government's defaulting on debt, or an international crisis are all significant possibilities.

A prolonged correction would likely result in a shift from financial assets into tangible ones. Inflation would make real estate and metals more valuable. People have to realize that markets don't go up and up, and hopefully that realization won't be completely devastating for those who have most of their assets in the equities market. In the future there may be a number of funds that will offer the public greater use of different instruments and strategies. International investing will be a great growth area. I foresee a new wave of internationally focused funds that can invest on the short side and in international derivatives.

◆

## TACTICAL ASSET ALLOCATORS

### *"I believe our kind of investing is the next wave."*

TONY RYAN *manages investments for New Money trading firm Pan-Agora, which uses quantitative strategies to bet on a dizzying array of securities opportunities around the world and manages some $15 billion.*

PanAgora uses global tactical asset allocation strategies in stocks, bonds, cash, and currencies. We have about $2 billion invested in international fixed income, $2 billion in equities, and additional funds in other investments.

We're in and out of the market on a monthly basis. We allocate our clients' funds around the world using various indexing strategies, trying to match or beat the performance of that index. We're active about country selection and passive once we've implemented the strategy. Since our investment strategy isn't buy-and-hold oriented, we never forget about currency risk—the possibility that our stock investments might go up at the same time as the currency of the country in which we're invested is devalued. Investors can lose all of their profits and more in a currency devaluation.

We aim for a target of 60 percent of our clients' assets invested in equities, including domestic equities. Since we're index investors, we can't invest in stocks that aren't included in an index. Indexes we use include the U.S. Standard & Poor's (S&P) 500, Morgan Stanley's European and Far Eastern (EAFE) index, and fixed-income indexes such as the Salomon Brothers' World Government Bond Index. There are also individual indexes for stocks and bonds that we track in various countries, such as Germany, the U.K., France, Australia, and Canada.

Although we run mutual funds and are regulated by the Securities and Exchange Commission (SEC), we don't actually buy stocks and bonds if we can help it. We would rather buy the futures of those instruments on various futures markets. Most government bonds of major countries are traded on futures exchanges, either within the borders of those countries or somewhere else. A number of European fixed-income futures are traded on the London Futures Exchange (LIFFE). It's much more cost-effective and efficient to trade a future than the underlying cash instrument because when you buy a future, you can use a lot more margin than you could if you were buying the actual instrument—and that means you can buy a lot more of whatever it is you wish to invest in.

In addition to buying fixed-income and equity exposure through the futures markets, we also buy currency forwards—like futures—at the same time.

I believe our kind of investing is the next wave of investing. The growth of the derivatives markets is extremely important to our business and to the success the world markets have had in handling the new capital flows. Obviously, we support the growth of the use of derivatives. Regulators have to make these instruments more readily available, but they also have to realize that the derivatives markets are growing faster than stock markets. It's not just a trend, it's here to stay. We're going to see institutional investors increasingly approach the market in an international or global fashion. Because of the derivatives markets, you don't need a lot of capital to invest abroad. We're right at the tip of the iceberg.

TIM MECKEL *is the international money manager for the legendary New Money firm, California-based First Quadrant. First Quadrant is an outstanding example of a new style of fund investing mostly in futures, especially overseas.*

We have about $15 billion under management currently and have taken in about $7 billion in the last five years. We have close to 45 clients, including 18 who trade internationally. We don't run any commingled funds, and each portfolio is individually weighted with different benchmarks, styles, and ranges.

We're a very quantitative firm with no subjective override. Basically we shift between asset classes around the world using listed futures and options. We'll combine stocks with bond indexes and hedge with currency forwards, though we don't make any pure currency plays or invest in commodities or metals.

We've developed 18 different country models to determine the relative attractiveness of stocks, bonds, and cash in each country. Then we link that to a global framework to determine which asset classes are the most attractive within a country—stocks versus bonds, for instance—and between countries. Our job isn't made any easier by regulators. We have 18 countries and only five authorized equity futures markets. We hope regulators will open up more futures markets as soon as possible since it's much easier and cheaper for us to buy futures than to assemble asset classes by buying the underlying stock.

It's ironic that U.S. investors haven't taken more advantage of international investments since we're very advanced in terms of what's going on. If you take Japan, the U.K., and France, three countries very active in international finance, we're still about five years ahead of them in terms of the markets where we invest and the information and techniques we apply. In Germany you can virtually forget about quantitative investments for the next five to 10 years—the big German banks just don't take it seriously. And Switzerland has just started to look at performance measurement.

---◆---

## SMALL INVESTOR ASSET MANAGEMENT

### *"This is one of a few firms for the small investor."*

JOHN BOWEN *is president of Reinhardt Werba Bowen, a California-based New Money management and financial planning firm.*

We don't believe in superior stock selection. We believe the market reflects all known information, so we offer the customer a series of funds that allow him various degrees of risk and reward. We put together instruments with dissimilar price movements— like stocks and bonds—that reduce risk while maintaining or increasing the reward.

We call this kind of investing strategic asset management. This is one of a few firms that specializes in strategic asset management money management, in both this country and overseas, for the retail investor. We began as a full-service financial planning firm but in the late 1980s decided to move in this direction. Applying academic thinking to investing is still not a popular concept, but we're not inventing anything. We're managing $400 million now, so there's obviously a need for what we're providing.

We don't actually manage money ourselves, though we manage the portfolio. We offer funds developed by such efficient market-oriented managers as Rex Sinquefield, president of Dimensional Fund Advisors. Rex runs some $10 billion, mostly for institutions that invest using some of the strategies we're offering to individual customers.

We tell individual investors that they can't hope to beat the market. Instead, they ought to invest in a blend of different asset classes that offer different risk and reward patterns. Then they can choose how much risk and reward they want.

———————◆———————

## MARKET TIMING RESEARCH

### *"We stay aware of economic trends that can cause the Fed to tighten."*

TIM HAYES *is senior international strategist at Ned Davis Research, Venice, Florida.*

We have three rules: Don't fight the tape, don't fight the Federal Reserve, and beware of the crowd at the extremes.

We watch closely what the Fed is doing. We stay in line with interest rate trends and monetary trends. The old adage is that money trends move markets, and we believe in that adage. We stay aware of economic trends that can cause the Fed to tighten.

We're macro in our approach, top-down, looking at the big picture first. Ned Davis was an analyst at JC Bradford, the regional broker, before starting this research firm in 1980. He really wanted to bring the computer into technical analysis, and he felt in the 1980s he would be able to do that. Today we sell research to many big institutions throughout the country. Ned Davis is known as a trend follower, a market timer, and he addresses that question from time to time. People will say you can't time the stock market, can't move in and out, but we've done a lot of studies to show the value of market timing. We've shown that if you can just miss the worst days, you're possibly better off than if you catch the best days. That's what much of our research is aimed at. There are a lot of clichés in this business, such as "Let your profits run" and "Cut losses short." But we think market timing keeps investors in the big moves because it's based on the action of the market itself. Once your indicators start breaking down, you're out.

We have all kinds of different indicators. We have an indicator, for instance, that bases itself off the S&P 500. When the S&P reverses by a certain amount, we get out. Ned correctly got our clients out of the market well before the crash of 1987. We realize you can't call a top or bottom, but you can make calls that will get you into 90 percent of an advance or decline, and that's what we try to do.

I don't know how you can invest overseas much without using our kind of investing. If you want to invest in markets where you don't know the culture or the language, you have to try to buy the broad market move. Of course, you have to be able to trust the data. Internationally, we offer a lot of relative strength data comparing one market to another. Markets tend to be correlated very closely these days, and market moves tend to be global in scope. You try to get into them when they're just getting underway.

———————◆———————

## FUNDAMENTAL TIMER

*"The best indicator is the Fed."*

TIM CLARK *manages a $600 million global fund for New York-based Zweig Securities.*

When I started in 1985, we had a total of 25 people and $300 billion under management. Now we have some $10 billion under management. We have all kinds of funds: open- and closed-end, hedge, and pension.

Our management is based on a market timing model that features three main areas. The first is monetary conditions, or the overall liquidity in the economy. The best indicator is the Fed and what it's trying to do in response to the real economy's needs. If the economy is getting stronger, then more and more money is needed in the real economy and interest rates will rise, leaving less money available for stocks and bonds. If the economy gets weaker, more money is available for financial investments. That's why the stock market is always looking six months ahead. Often a poor time to invest is when companies are reporting top earnings. That's when economic liquidity tends to start drying up.

Momentum is another key area we monitor. We're not trying to be smarter than the market. We try to respect it as much as possible. The trend is your friend, as they say. If it's going higher, we tend to add exposure.

The final area we track is investor sentiment, and that's hard to get a handle on. We'll use mutual fund cash-to-asset ratios to determine how much cash investors have sitting on the sidelines. We'll also use short interest and odd-lot short interest, but that's less valid now because of program trading and other trading techniques.

We try to time markets, but that doesn't mean we take chances. We're risk-averse. The whole idea is to preserve capital in down markets so we'll be able to participate in the up moves. It does no good to be up 20 percent one year and then down 20 percent the next. We try to manage our risk overseas by using active-currency hedging models. As for stocks and bonds, unlike most other mutual funds, we'll go from 100 percent invested to nothing, with the residual invested in cash. The mix of stocks and bonds to cash is determined by quantitative timing models.

I don't make extensive use of over-the-counter derivatives, though more funds are using them. A Wall Street firm will sell you a participation in an index—domestic or foreign—for instance. Those opportunities are now available to all of us.

With respect to trading, there are SEC rules that make it difficult to move in and out of certain instruments, and we have to take them into account. But we're certainly not a buy-and-hold fund. That's not our strategy.

◆

## HEDGE FUND CONSULTING

*"I recommend hedge fund managers—equity managers who use proprietary trading techniques to capture superior performance."*

E. LEE HENNESSEE *is the director of Republic Securities hedge fund program, recommending hedge fund managers for domestic and international clients. She has researched some 800 hedge funds over the years.*

There is a lot of misunderstanding about the managers we categorize. I don't recommend managers who specialize in futures. I recommend hedge fund managers—equity managers who use proprietary trading techniques to capture superior performance. The rule I use is that if more than 15 percent of a fund's capital is in worldwide derivatives, in currencies or options derivatives, then I define them as macro hedge funds.

The field is evolving. In the 1950s when hedge funds started to become popular, they went long and short just in the stock market. The positions were hedged, and that's why they were called hedge funds. But as technology and new investment vehicles evolve, some equity managers who have been around for a while have begun to feel comfortable with the more esoteric weightings. The strategies have changed as new instruments became available. Options were the first derivatives to hit the Street, back in the early 1970s. Stock options came first, then index options. You could use the options as a bet on the market or as a hedge. Stock futures indexes started out for the purpose of hedging, as did currency futures and forwards. But these days many funds invest to take directional bets, not as a hedge.

In addition to the funds themselves, there has been a proliferation of fund of funds. I've collected information on some 250 fund of funds with minimums as low as $3,000, but most fund of funds have minimums more like $100,000 to $1 million. As I've studied and been exposed to these markets I've seen the business evolve, and my approach has, too, to the selection criteria I use. I'm first interested in the investment process of the fund, then in past performance, third in who they are—name recognition—and, fourth, fees and charges.

This is a young field, and most of the funds, especially the international funds, don't have a long track record. That's why my clients come to me. They want diversification of management and style. They want someone to monitor their investments and sort it out for them.

DON HARDY *tracks hedge funds for Washington-based Frank Russell Co.*

Hedge funds are a kind of unique vehicle. They can operate on both sides of the market, whereas most investors operate solely on the long side of the market. The first one was set up by A.W. Jones in the 1950s and they have grown tremendously since then.

It's a sophisticated investment. People who set up hedge funds are not entry-level investment managers. They tend to set up hedge funds to manage their own or their family's money or maybe the money of friends. The way they're set up, they can take incentive compensation so they can make a large amount of money for themselves and for others if they do well. The incentives tend to make the investor and the investment manager partners, and that's different from the way mutual funds are structured with fee-based services. Some of these hedge funds are set up as limited partnerships, and the hedge fund manager puts in his own money. Since capital is on the line, he is going to share the pain as well as the gain.

Hedge funds are typically equity-oriented. Since they're private investment partnerships, they can be sold only to wealthy, accredited investors—sophisticated investors.

Hedge funds at the end of the day are a very opportunistic vehicle. Many of them are unstructured and take opportunities where they can find them. But it takes a certain level of investment sophistication to put your money with an opportunistic type of vehicle.

Operating on the short side of the market is tricky because the potential for loss is greater. The stock market's long-term bias is upward, and equity values should reflect that growth. If you make an investment and it's an untimely one, you can basically sit on your hands until the upward momentum bails you out. But if you're selling short, you can't count on that momentum. You don't have the underlying forces working in your favor. Also, most of the research being done is on the long side—on what's a good investment, not what's a bad one. Short sellers are out there on their own, doing their own research. Selling short as well as long is a risky strategy, though the rewards can be substantial.

◆

## INTERNATIONAL HEDGER

### *"We can honestly tell clients who use these strategies that they're not subject to the ups and downs of the stock market."*

WALTER NOEL *is an investment management consultant and a partner of the Fairfield-Greenwich Group, which runs a high-performing group of funds.*

For our funds, we use nontraditional market-neutral strategies, which themselves use equity and derivative products. We also find fund managers on behalf of wealthy individuals, most of them foreign. Nominally we ask for investments of $100,000, but usually much more than that is invested. The reason is that limited partnerships, which are the way performance-based funds are offered in this country, are highly restricted vehicles. SEC rules state that you can't offer the same strategies to more than 99 people. Then another fund has to be set up, and it can't offer the strategies used in the first fund. Naturally, since it takes a lot of time, effort, and intellect to set up a successful investment strategy, most of our top fund investors either invest just their own money or mostly have overseas clients. Overseas, you can offer more than 99 investors the same investment strategies at one time.

The SEC is trying to limit fraud and losses because of risky investments. But these days, top managers may actually be more conservative, by using a variety of new instruments, than the traditional kind of mutual fund investment. What happens if the market moves down and mutual funds are hit by a wave of liquidations? It could have a snowball effect. We think we're a very cautious group. What we do is something that is particularly good for the low-risk investor, the person who wants to invest and have low volatility. This investor, because of our business, is necessarily outside the United States.

The typical cross-border nest-egg-style investor cannot sleep well unless we're exercising extreme care, and for us that means investing in a good, strong, equity portfolio that smooths out the bumps and jolts of normal market performance. To do this, we use hedging and arbitrage techniques. We can honestly tell clients who use these strategies that they're not subject to the ups and downs of the stock market.

We take the market timing out of getting into the market. We use hedging and arbitrage techniques to do that. By hedging, I mean going long and short on the same securities or group of securities. One example of this strategy in this country was when we bought Bank of America, which we felt was a good buy, and then shorted the bank index. It worked very well—we made money on the stock purchase—and we were a lot safer than had we purchased the stock without the hedge. We were happy with our profit and our position, and we didn't look back to say we missed a chance to do even better because we knew if the market went down and pulled Bank of America with it, we could have done worse.

We've wound up concentrating on these low-risk transactions because we have to know how to please clients. We don't want to be embarrassed in a sell-off or crash. A lot of our business matured after we weathered the 1987 crash. I was able to tell people they made money during the crash—they didn't lose anything. We're giving our clients a unique investment service, but one that's out of reach to most American investors because of the regulatory situation. George Soros's success has been out of the reach of Americans because he didn't want to go through the hassle of setting up a fund for American investors that would pass SEC scrutiny. Michael Steinhardt went through with the exercise and then found that the trading rules imposed by the SEC in the equity markets were such that it was impossible for him to pursue his strategies. He has to move in and out of stocks faster than the SEC allows.

DIXON BOARDMAN *runs a fund of funds as well as a single fund, Optima.*

We have several international funds including our Optima Global fund and an international futures fund. We've been in business five years and have $500 million under management. I was a broker with Kidder Peabody for a number of years. Finally, I began to notice that there was a group of people who year in and year out consistently made money, and most of them were in hedge funds. The returns were so consistent and so compelling that it triggered me to do a comprehensive study of the industry.

There are some hedge funds that have huge volatility, but we think that by putting managers together, and mixing and matching managers and portfolios, we can take out a fairly substantial portion of the risk. We have never had a down quarter. I believe an investor's money is safer with us than invested in conventional mutual funds.

Our industry is in its infancy; I think that more and more banks will adopt a fund-of-funds kind of approach as time goes by. We already have been approached by a major U.S. bank to show them what we're doing, and we have a relationship with a major overseas bank.

We also run private accounts and separate institutional accounts. The biggest argument against a fund of funds is double fees. That's why the kinds of funds we offer can't be made available to the general public in the United States for regulatory reasons. But our customers are knowledgeable people who like having the exposure to the smart money guys out there. As far as performance is concerned, it's like using a cannon against Bambi. We'll win every time.

There are so many restrictions on conventional funds. You're restricted on the amount of money you can have in any one security, you can't invest in derivatives, and you can't use hedging techniques because of the short-short rules. The most important difficulty is that if you're running a mutual fund, you have to maintain a relatively substantial cash balance to stay liquid for redemptions. The more cash you have sitting idle, the more you erode performance. With a mutual fund, you can't use leverage in a traditional sense. The top manager who can use leverage is always going to do better than the top manager who can't.

---◆---

## International Equity Arbitrage

### *"Derivatives are the wave of the future."*

BOB GORDON, *a former Oppenheimer & Co. partner, now runs his own New Money firm, Twenty-First Securities Corp. A cutting-edge money pro, Gordon seeks out international tax and regulatory arbitrages to lock into "riskless" profit.*

The few of those who understand tax implications of regulations—that everything is not treated the same in every country—know that's what drives the equity swap market. The easiest example is to look at German markets. A German dividend of $1.40 is worth only a dollar to a U.S. investor. Therefore, a dividend on a German stock is worth one thing to a U.S. taxpayer and quite another one to a German taxpayer. This is what the equity swap business is driven by.

Let's consider Canada. As of January 1, 1994, a Canadian citizen can't take a deduction for paying out a dividend when he's short a stock. Meanwhile, in the United States, when we're short a stock and pay out a dividend, we do get an adjustment. If I'm short for 46 days or more, I get a deduction. We get a break for the money we paid out, but a Canadian investor won't. The Canadian tax policies have made the U.S. investor the most tax-efficient investor.

I also do hedges or arbitrages with a foreign security—say, sovereign government Eurobonds that have no risk and have been returning over 20 percent to my clients. We buy a sovereign country's debt and then hedge the risk with bond futures. We can return the 20 percent because of a mispricing between the bonds and the futures.

In the future, countries developing now won't just build stock markets. They'll have futures and options markets coming on line at the same time. With derivatives, you don't have to worry about settlement, clearing, or currency problems. Derivatives are the wave of the future.

---

◆

---

# NEURAL NET TRADER

## *"People will bet twice as much, ten times as much."*

CASEY KLIMASAUSKAS *is cofounder of a firm that uses artificial intelligence software to design trading strategies. The firm also sells its NeuralWare software, which is capable of learning trade patterns and then detecting those patterns in actual trading encounters.*

Life is not fair. I've sat in front of screens, and I've watched people sell with obvious foreknowledge. Or sometimes people will hear about or detect a big move: Salomon is selling this, Kidder Peabody is selling that. Now how is that different from knowing a month before it happens that some big computer manufacturer won't meet its profit margins?

Insider trading is like prohibition. Basically you're trying to say that there are certain kinds of information you can't have or act on. It says if you become particularly successful, you're doing something illegal.

Money, power, and prestige tend to motivate people. In this society, we continually pass laws that demotivate people. I think the regulators will have to confront computer trading sooner or later, and I also think they'll try to crack down on it. But if you crack down on trading on individual securities—and it would be extremely hard to crack down on anything else, say, currencies or bond trading—they'll just chase the money away. The technology is coming, and it's going to be used internationally. What the regulators will probably end up doing is chasing the money into derivatives.

The new kinds of trading software are going to increase current market trends. Velocity will increase. If you're sure of your bet, you can make a ton of money, and that means money will be attracted to the market using the new software and the new strategies. People will bet twice as much, 10 times as much.

JOHN LOOFBOURROW *a former Salomon Brothers executive, now builds and markets neural net software. He also trades for his own account with a system of his own design and predicts that such sophisticated software will soon change the way money pros invest around the world.*

Neural nets work like this. Pretend you're a spider on the edge of a very smooth pond, trying to decide if an insect dropped in. If you have enough feet on the surface, you can tell about the insect. If you have wind and ripples, the neural net will pull the pattern out of the noise. It's basically matching patterns, surfaces. Take any point in time, daily for the last five years. Now you've got a surface. Points on the curve and time make up a three-dimensional surface. You also need historical data. That's how you train the net. It will pick up patterns from the historical data and then detect similar patterns or variations in patterns as they occur or before they occur.

It can pick up these patterns faster than you or I can. That was the insight I came away with watching a trader at Salomon Brothers, where I worked. He bought the bonds because he sensed he'd seen that pattern before. Pricing patterns can be compressed or elongated, and the neural net will still pick them up.

All the neural net does is isolate patterns. I've been trading one of the three big car companies for a while, and invariably before some major movement the stock goes long or short. You know something's happening, and if you follow the trend, you can get in on it. In the future, I'm not sure the little guy is going to be able to compete in these markets, but I'm not sure an even playing field is needed anymore. The complexity of this software will tend to deemphasize the role of the intermediary and expand the role of those institutions that possess the requisite software. A lot of funds have the software and technology these days.

---◆---

## NEW MONEY: DIVERSIFICATION AND REFLATION

*"Eventually funds will start to come out that offer more asset class-variety."*

SCOTT LUMMER *heads up a fast-growing consulting group for Chicago-based Ibbotson.*

It's hard to tell what's international and what isn't among funds since many funds will call themselves international but still be heavily invested in the United States. An investor who wants to place a certain amount of assets overseas better find out just how much of the fund's assets are actually outside the United States.

One predictable way of investing abroad is through index funds, which must maintain certain amounts of equity exposure in certain countries. But investing abroad doesn't, by itself, guarantee adequate diversification. Diversification involves much more than just equity investing. Even balanced funds that give exposure to both stocks and bonds aren't giving real diversification across asset classes.

Eventually funds will start to come out that offer more asset-class variety, but for now the average investor still has to be his own fund of funds. He has to make certain economic decisions about where to invest and then follow through.

**ROBERT ARNOTT** *is president and chief executive of First Quadrant. He is the author of more than 40 professional articles as well as the first and second editions of* Active Asset Allocation *(Probus Press).*

There are only about a dozen firms that do what we would consider tactical asset allocation on a domestic basis and only a handful that are using the strategy internationally. Global tactical asset allocation (GTAA) has a very good record. Our process has been live for four and half years, and we've been 400 basis points over international indexes on average during that time. But GTAA isn't an easy strategy to implement, and maybe that's why it's not more popular. It takes a contrarian approach to the markets, and that takes patience. But there's nothing in the data to support the view that GTAA has been anything less than a profitable way of investing.

We tend to use futures rather than underlying stocks and

bonds to shift assets around because futures are cheaper to trade and the taxes are much less. We did $75 billion worth of futures trades in the last two years on behalf of our institutional customers. We're mostly in the institutional business, though we have some limited partnerships for smaller investors as well as a couple of wealthy investors who invest with us.

We're considering setting up a mutual fund. I think it's naive of many mutual funds not to use the full panoply of instruments and asset classes available to them. Unfortunately, for mutual funds, the IRS' short-short rule constrains how fast you can get in and out of instruments. Too fast, and you lose your tax benefits as a fund. With institutional clients we don't have to worry about the short-short rule. But that's a clear example of how regulations make it difficult for the average investor to gain access to modern markets and strategies.

I think we're riding a wave of interest. And as a firm, we plan to employ more instruments and asset classes in the future. For instance, if we see a meaningful acceleration in inflation, I think we would take a hard look at bringing out a real estate or metals fund.

———————◆———————

## NEW MONEY RISKS

*"What's true for Morgan Stanley is probably not possible for Joe Smith."*

DOMINIC CASSERLEY *is a former member of the Brady Commission and director, McKinsey & Co.*

There are many different ways to access the markets, but two facts are still constant. The first is that you make attractive risk-adjusted returns only if you have some market advantage—better information or better skills. And it is unlikely that the individual investor is going to have that. Second, the investor should be diversified and invested according to his or her risk appetite. The days when you invest just in American securities are completely gone.

The crux of the problem for individuals is that most financial markets are still pretty inefficient. If a market is not perfectly efficient, there are opportunities to make attractive risk-adjusted returns. But remember, what's true for Morgan Stanley is probably not possible for Joe Smith.

The risk is that an individual looks at what a major institution is able to achieve and thinks, "I can do that too." But here the institution has many advantages—more information and more ways of trading, including the mathematical investment strategies. Add to that reduced transactions costs and on-line trading opportunities, and you have many advantages over the individual investor. It's probably simplistic to focus on just one.

------------◆------------

## WHAT REMAINS THE SAME

### *"All these funds still trade through Wall Street."*

HOWARD SILVERMAN *is a top Wall Street broker and money manager who often writes on financial industry topics.*

Historically, there have been two fundamental schools of thought in securities investments: fundamental and technical. Now there's a quantitative school as well, based on analyzing groups of securities all at once. The computer has changed the way the securities industry is shaped and changed the way instruments are valued, marketed, and multiplied.

But with all the new funds and new strategies, one thing

hasn't changed. All of these funds, private or public, hedge funds or international funds, still trade mostly through Wall Street firms. So although a lot of new things are going on with mutual funds, the actual way these funds buy and sell their securities hasn't changed. They still use Wall Street.

The ability to transfer that risk comes from the computer, but risk hasn't changed either. In 1987 there was something called portfolio insurance that was supposed to protect mutual funds and pension funds from market downturns. Now, in the early 1990s, derivatives are supposed to do the same thing, and it's true that derivatives are more complicated than portfolio insurance, but the hedge you're buying might be too big for the market. You think you can get out, but you can't. Funds have changed, but Wall Street hasn't.

# WHAT I LEARNED
◆

I did not originally intend to break out New Money from Big Money in this book. It was only as I spoke to more and more managers—experienced international players like Colonial's Dan Rie and PanAgora's Tony Ryan—that I began to see the pattern emerging: the use of the computer for market timing and international investing in a variety of instruments. The similarities between New Money managers running Big Money and hedge fund operators have to do in part with a way of seeing instruments. New Money managers in general see investments in aggregate, at least on occasion, and they pay attention to instruments other than stock. For New Money managers, investments need not be for the long term, and profits may be realized for reasons that have nothing to do with value. Of course, a good deal of passion swirls around this kind of investing. For Wall Street pros who want to protect their positions as gatekeepers of the physical exchange floor, stock trading is a paramount investment opportunity.

In the near term, international New Money investing is important to investors in what must eventually become a reflationary domestic environment. With Germany—Europe's economic engine—not quite overheating, it is likely that overseas markets offer investors an equity upside not nearly so certain in this country. Additionally, as Don Hardy points out (with appropriate cautions), hedge funds' ability to participate in short selling means that if there is a reflation domestically, those hedge funds with U.S. equity exposure may realize big profits. Hot Money funds (see Chapter Five), too, can participate in the short side of the market. Investors who can't afford hedge funds might do well to investigate managed futures funds.

My talks with market timers and strategists like Ned Davis's Tim Hayes convinced me that there is bottom-line validity to at least some of the strategies and tools employed. Of course the investor can use principles of market timing through asset allocation. A country in a recession is obviously in a recession, and a portfolio can be weighted to acknowledge that fact. A country at the top of a red-hot recovery probably cannot sustain low interest rates for long (especially if that country is subject to central banking policies). Comprehending business cycles and acting on that knowledge is not, or should not be, considered a radical procedure.

A last point: Computers will continue to commoditize markets, if NeuralWare's Casey Klimasauskas is right about the impact of technology on investments. New Money investors will increasingly have access to new kinds of market and government data that allow money pros to move quickly and act on hunches or in accordance with computer-driven strategies. Like it or not, the future of investing in a fiat-money environment is one of more market velocity, not less.

Given the difficulties that investors face on Wall Street—

difficulties that won't soon be alleviated, as market pro Howard Silverman points out in his comment on New Money risk—an investor's best weapons would seem to involve business cycle macroallocation.

# INVESTMENT SUMMARY
◆

## NEW MONEY: DIFFICULTIES OF DIVERSIFYING

◆ Diversification is a necessary part of modern investors' portfolios, but there are still relatively few ways an investor can diversify internationally. Big Money mutual funds offer some investment opportunity, but they are often rigid and one-dimensional vehicles. New Money funds are better but still suffer from difficulties inherent in the country's regulated financial structure.

◆ Diversification is more easily achievable within New Money funds that involve flexible investments across asset classes, not just within instruments. But New Money still doesn't make maximum use of markets or investment techniques.

◆ True international diversification demands a richness of strategies and the use of innovative investment vehicles. New Money investments are just starting to exploit these opportunities.

## WHAT THE INVESTOR CAN DO

◆ To ensure maximum equity diversification, the investor can seek out other kinds of investments than Big Money. New Money funds that make use of futures, options, and even commodities or metals are choices the internationally oriented investor might consider.

♦ Investigate hedge fund alternatives. Although hedge funds are restricted from offering their services to more than 99 individuals at a time, it is possible that certain hedge fund strategies may eventually find their way into public funds. As competition continues to heat up in this sector, minimums may come down, allowing smaller investors more access to this investing arena.

♦ Be aware of the shortcomings of both New Money and Big Money strategies, and learn about domestic rules and regulations that restrict Big Money and New Money from offering true-asset class diversification. Investors with the wherewithal should certainly consider the international hedge fund option for at least a small portion of their portfolio, bearing in mind that the hot hedge fund manager may have at least some of the order-flow intelligence possessed by top Wall Street dealing firms.

## New Money Problems That Remain

♦ Private and public New Money, like much Big Money, is still mostly restricted to equity markets, and most of it still trades through Wall Street. Despite their growth, hedge funds are mostly domestic and still mostly oriented toward stock and options purchases. Much of the one-dimensional nature of hedge funds has to do with the difficulty that their managers face in conforming to different regulatory structures. To trade stock domestically, they must conform to certain SEC guidelines; to trade financial futures and commodities, they must conform to Commodity Futures Trading Commission (CFTC) rules. Most won't try to do both. The ones that do often operate overseas.

♦ Private New Money, especially unregulated hedge funds, can sell short and use leverage. Public New Money (innovative mutual funds) can't use much leverage and therefore sacrifices gains. Additionally, public New Money must abide by public fund fee structures, which don't allow for much in the way of incentives. Much of the payment structure for public Big Money and public New Money remains the same. The difference is that public New Money takes advantage of more instruments around the world and sometimes invests in more asset classes.

♦ Most U.S.-style Big Money can't sell short—in the classic sense, anyway—but that's what private money is good at. In a reflationary environment, hedge funds especially are worth looking into. But even the larger, public, New Money funds are likely to weather inflation better than Big Money, with its long equity emphasis. But true deflation-reflation hedging lies, at least to some degree, outside the securities markets—in Hot Money, as we will see in the next chapter.

## CHAPTER FIVE

# HOT MONEY

◆

## Futures, Derivatives, and Currencies

Futures traders are used to thinking in terms of groups of instruments and comfortable with hedging and other kinds of trading strategies. A good (and at least relatively honest) commodities investment adviser or futures-oriented hedge fund on a roll in the international markets can make big profits for customers. But it's true that futures investing in this country remains a risky play. The almost pathological clubbiness of the industry's top players, increasingly buttressed by regulatory authority, precludes the competition that would give the investor the kind of pricing and service that stock-oriented Big Money and Wall Street have benefited from.

The result of the incestuous relationship between the industry's main players and its main regulator, the Commodity Futures Trading Commission (CFTC), is that the industry and the consumer are losing, as I write, yet another opportunity to play commodities as a reflationary hedge. Until managed futures fees come down as real competition blows through the industry, the offerings by commodity trading advisers will often remain flawed

155

and expensive. Futures commission merchants add another layer of complexity and expense to the already cumbersome procedures.

The whole mess is topped off by Chicago's pit trading where gravel-voiced traders scream at one another and undermine, when possible, any attempt to open up the industry, through true electronic trading. What's the result? Electronic futures trading may take root elsewhere in the world before it will in Chicago—just as electronic stock trading is making more progress in former Eastern Bloc countries than it is in New York.

This is too bad because futures products will play a bigger and bigger role in the financial industry—at least among institutional players. Commodity futures are not derivatives in the sense that a product is being bought and sold (though not usually delivered). But futures, especially financial futures that make a bet on an underlying product (stock, to begin with), were among the first and most popular derivative instruments traded in large quantity. As more and more financial bets are made on more products through the use of the computer, the model provided by the futures industry could well prove more sympathetic to modern finance—for the larger financial industry players—than that provided by Wall Street's rigid stock industry, embodied by the New York Stock Exchange (NYSE) and the Street's largest brokerage wirehouses.

However, it's also true that according to several of my insiders, the managed futures industry is shrinking even as I write. It may even be possible that one or more of the insiders I spoke to about the industry for this section will be out of business by the time this book is published. The crux of the problem is that the industry is far more convenient for the large investor than for the small.

As always you have to go back in time to figure out how the futures industry got to where it is today and why it is still the poor sister, in terms of reputation and investor attractiveness, of establishment stock trading.

Futures trading was less reputable than stock trading because equity trading was located in New York and dealt with the funding of corporations rather than the hedging of grain and meat. Another reason is that there wasn't so much money in futures. It was considered to be the province of small-time hustlers living off weather conditions. Farmers were and still are suspicious of the manipulations that occur in the futures markets. But a famous deal struck over lunch by two of the nation's top financial regulators at Washington, D.C.'s Monocle restaurant in 1982 (The Securities and Exchange's [SEC] John Shad and the CFTC's Philip Johnson) gave the futures industry oversight over noncash financial markets. The deal almost immediately ignited the financial revolution that has swept over Wall Street. Once institutions could bet on groups of instruments instead of individual instruments, the possibilities of computerized investing were unleashed—though mostly for pension plans, not individual investors in mutual funds.

In fact, this is the weakness of the industry. Because of its history, futures just aren't set up to accommodate the small investor. In order to generate a derivatives product, futures exchanges set up pits, and pits are expensive to create and maintain. Additionally, futures work on generous margining and therefore individual investors usually don't have the wherewithal to sustain their investments when the market swings against them even a little.

Managed futures are a valiant try at converting what is essentially a creative derivatives market for institutions to individual customers. But the futures industry ultimately will have to do a lot more maturing to accommodate the average investor looking for a plain-vanilla inflationary hedge.

Still, this much is true: In the modern era of marketshock, as pretechnology fiscal levers like tax policy, Federal Reserve actions, and tariffs collide with computerized capital, economies are bound to fluctuate. As the deflation-reflation cycle grinds on, managed futures, at least in theory, provide an appropriate hedge.

Unfortunately, the better managers—those that will survive the current shakeout—are often only available to wealthier investors. In any event, the small investor, frustrated in his search for a performance-oriented futures pool or fund, can also consider direct purchases of metals or real estate as a reflationary hedge. Or he can take his chances with a leveraged commodity index play on, say, the New York Futures Exchange. None of this is completely satisfactory. But in the era of marketshock, what constitutes a completely safe bet?

———————◆———————

## OVERVIEW

### "We trade currencies, options, fixed income, and futures, as well as equity."

PAUL NATHAN *is co-head of trading at powerful, family-owned Swiss bank Julius Baer.*

We're private bankers, and we want to give our wealthy clients the best opportunities available, worldwide. Basically we have a 24-hour trading operation at the bank. Our customers are high-net-worth individuals and fund managers. We provide trading services and we're market makers. If customers wish, we keep them posted on a frequent basis as to the disposition of their book. We trade currencies, options, fixed income, and futures, as well as equity. We also trade with other banks and with fund managers.

We trade our currencies through the interbank exchange aided by computer systems provided to us by big information vendors.

International trading and derivatives trading is becoming more popular. People have known how to invest in fixed income and equities, and now they're starting to realize they can do variations of all this overseas. Technology is advancing at an extremely rapid pace. Off-exchange trading for currencies is becoming more and more liquid; for fixed-income products, the liquidity on an exchange is higher. Markets find their best trading environment through fulfilling certain basic criteria. The first thing is liquidity. Can you trade an instrument when you like as often as you like? Then there's slippage. How long does it take you to trade the instrument and how close can you trade to the price you wanted to get when you decided on the trade? The third criterion is spreads. A tighter market means more trading and more liquidity. The last criterion is the cost of doing business.

Exchanges, for instance, establish credit and guarantee trades. That's important in the futures industry, where you have lots of smaller players who could not get an aggressive line of credit from a bank. In the interbank market, your participants are large, creditworthy individuals and institutions. But no matter what instruments are traded where, global trading in both the derivatives and cash markets will continue to grow. It can't be stopped. It's part of the globalization of industry and capital flows.

———————◆———————

## FUTURES FUND OF FUNDS

### *"We try to create market-neutral, hedged positions."*

GLENN DUBIN, *with partner Henry Swieca, runs one of the country's hotter commodity operations.*

Our competitive advantage is that we've been able to identify successful traders early in their careers. That's what people pay us to do—find these rising stars.

There is an enormous amount of liquidity in the world, and the liquidity is being directed into the markets through this mutual fund mania. There's so much capital looking for attractive investment returns that there is a self-fulfilling prophecy of the kind that happened in Japan. Liquidity continued to fuel the boom until the 1990s, when the fundamentals weren't there. Investors have to adjust to the environment we're in—an equity environment in which prices are going higher. It's a stock market mania based on an enormous pool of cash.

There has been a proliferation of new instruments and products over the years. Whenever there's an influx of supply, there are always market inefficiencies, so we try to create market-neutral, hedged positions exploiting the inefficiencies within the marketplace. We'll look at equity in emerging markets. We'll also put on a synthetic, market-neutral position, one where you've bought a convertible bond—one you can convert to equity—while also selling short at the same time.

From my perspective, creating multi-adviser funds, I can choose the best managers in the world to work with, the ones with the greatest investment success. They can be everywhere all at once—cash, futures, and options—but domestic U.S. investors can't take part in that. I think the government's objective is to protect U.S. investors, but to some extent the regulatory environment is so restrictive that it harms rather than protects investors by not giving them access to the best traders and advisers around the world.

◆

## FUTURES MANAGEMENT

*"We believe markets make big trends
on occasion, and we try to capitalize
on these trends."*

IRWIN BERGER *is a director of trading for SJO Inc., a futures shop using international techniques learned from top trader Richard Dennis.*

I used to be an undergraduate business teacher teaching marketing research. Then a friend got a job with the famous trader Richard Dennis, and after Dennis decided to stop trading, my friend wanted to continue. Since I had experience through my studies and my own trading, I went into business with him.

Dennis was a technical trader. There is technical trading in the stock market, but it's popular in the futures market because it provides discipline and makes the trends easier to deal with. Since you're dealing with single instruments and, in commodities, with seasonal tendencies, it makes sense that the futures markets are cyclical. Heating oil and natural gas contracts tend to move up and down in price at certain times during the year.

We try to trade in a number of different markets. Ideally we would like to have uncorrelated markets like the grain market and currencies. It's difficult to make a living trading in just one market unless you get commissions. We get incentive fees with small management fees.

Our approach is technical. We believe markets make big trends on occasion, and we try to capitalize on these trends. Currency is the most liquid market for the type of trading we do. Then there are the other markets—the futures on the bond market and equities. But we don't trade straight stocks right now. We basically deal in the futures.

We are not a hedge fund in that we don't have the capabilities to trade equities. We don't have the licenses available. What George Soros is doing is trying to take advantage of any opportunity, and we'd like to be in that kind of position. We're not yet as diversified as we'd like to be.

You could say this industry of ours is still in its infancy. We intend to broaden ourselves beyond managed futures. There are so many markets that have taken off in the last five years—the cash currency markets, the overseas interest-rate markets. We're going to be players in all these markets, not only for our institutional accounts but for private money and our own account as well. We have clients from the United States and from overseas as well. Right now there are a lot of trading advisers—over 1,000 commodity trading advisers—but there are not a lot who specialize in trading all around the world.

**DOUG MITCHELL** *runs the hot money futures advisory firm of CCA Capital Management.*

I started as a futures trader for myself in 1973, always an off-floor trader. Today I have about $95 million under management, and the style I use is primarily technical trend following. This means setting up a mathematical model and then formulating rules, testing it on past history, and simulating past trading. Then you can go away and optimize your mathematical model. Trend following is complementary to the standard buy-and-hold strategy of stock managers in which you buy and then hang on until it's fairly valued and then you sell. Buy low and sell high. In trend following, the market has a price, and the price starts to rise—that's when we buy. We buy high and sell higher. It sounds simple, but obviously it's not that simple or everyone would be doing it.

The last couple of years we've done extremely well. Our best program, the global strategic program, is up 25 percent this year and 50 percent last year. We trade precious metals, currencies, agricultural products like soybeans, coffee, and orange juice, and long-term bonds—U.S., French, German, English, and Australian bonds.

Our services can help investors. If interest rates go up in the United States and an investor owns a lot of stocks, his portfolio could get hammered—but people like us can make a pile of money when the stock market goes down. As long as there is some sort of movement in the market, we'll make a profit.

In my opinion, futures funds like the one we run are overregulated by a factor of ten. The best fund managers, like Paul Tudor

Jones, won't even run money in the United States. They run only offshore funds. The regulators are all over us. People do audits of us all the time. We have to disclose our performance, and the cost is very high. The net effect is that we go through great hoops to comply, and after a while it's not cost-effective for either the customer or the manager.

An investor interested in combining management strategies in futures for strategic diversification could hire a trend follower who uses a computerized strategy, a niche asset trader who concentrates mostly on one commodity or financial instrument, and finally a discretionary trader. Those are the main futures strategies at the moment.

———— ◆ ————

## COMPETITIVE RATES

*"You'd have to find a heck of a good
trader to surmount the fees some of
these CTAs charge."*

DON KAREL *runs MRK with legendary futures trader Mark Ritchie. The two run the $14 million Investor's Advantage managed futures fund, which Karel calls the first futures fund to be priced for the investor rather than for the manager.*

I was a member of the Chicago Mercantile Exchange (Merc) for a number of years in the 1970s and 1980s, and that's where I met Mark Ritchie. Eventually we decided to put together a firm, MRK, and set up a fund, Investor's Advantage. We're trend investors, but we'll also take short-term profits. We're very disciplined in what we do because discipline is necessary to take a profit. We're also diversified into various classes—currencies, grains, and now some of the European fixed-income markets.

We don't take money to run ourselves, and we don't charge investors any up-front fee. We make our profit entirely based on our performance. We need to return the T-bill rate to the investor, or we get nothing.

Mark Ritchie's track record is amazing. He's had nothing but up years, a 40 percent profit-per-year average since 1987, and Investor's Advantage is based on Ritchie's ideas. What makes the system work are discipline and better ideas coming from continuous research. We work extremely hard for our money and are constantly refining what we do to keep up with changes in the world economic environment and in technology.

I'd never advise not to invest in a mutual fund, but I would say that futures have been proven to be an aid to a balanced portfolio. Right now it costs $250,000 to get into our fund, but we're going to be offering a fund that has a minimum of $50,000. It will be structured the same way as Investor's Advantage. The typical Commodity Trading Adviser (CTA) has to make 12 percent before a client makes a penny, and the typical CTA has to make 28 percent before the client's profit begins to exceed the CTA's on a percentage basis. We don't think that's fair based on the client's taking all the risk. It's his money. The average CTA obviously makes money on everything but trading. You'd have to find a heck of a good trader to surmount the fees some of these CTAs charge.

Out of logic, I would think that you want to be set up in a situation where you are a true partner with your trader when it comes to facing the world. If the CTA is working just for fees, I don't know what the incentive is to take risk. Our clients want us to take risks. Our problem is one of communication. We're a private fund, and the CFTC says we can't advertise rates, which means we have to get our message out by word of mouth. We have what we feel is the best vehicle in the industry, but nobody knows about it.

Brokerages won't sell our product because we won't give them any fees to do it. We could go public, which would allow us to advertise, but that costs hundreds of thousands of dollars. There are all the state laws, the blue sky laws, and they're different in every state. Many of these laws are archaic, and they're hurting investors. Times have changed. When I started running this business, I thought I would spend 20 percent of the time on the business stuff and 80 percent of the time marketing. Instead it's been the other way around. I'm spending most of my time on the day-to-day accounting and regulatory stuff. We're thinking about going offshore.

**MARK RITCHIE** *is the investment head of a managed futures fund, Investor's Advantage Fund, and a world-class commodities trader.*

Managed futures may be one of the best opportunities now because there is somewhat of a track record (if you don't count the fly-by-night artists—just the consistent and upstanding wing of the industry). Don Karel and I have talked about forming a consortium of straight-shooting CTAs, and we may do it. The questions about the industry are one reason I didn't get into managed futures earlier. I actually wondered if my legitimate track record could ever stack up to some of the numbers that some of these traders claim. I'm not sure how the average investor figures out who's honest. I suppose he or she could start with the book *Market Wizards*. I have more at stake in this business, but I used to tell people to stay out of it.

There are so many ways of trading futures. We trade on long-term and short-term trends. There's nothing magic about it. A better trader has a better picture. Most bad traders are mystic. Most good traders are machinelike and very disciplined.

More and more, the responsible wing of the managed futures industry is looking toward strategies that hit singles in lots of different markets, and that's why I'm optimistic about my own portfolio. People say we're experiencing volatility, but that's because we're not in quite enough markets yet. The more markets we trade in, the more we'll smooth out that volatility.

———————◆———————

## DISCOUNT FUTURES

### *"The computer has been a major part of this phenomenal growth."*

CAROL DANNENHAUER *is director of managed accounts for discount futures broker, Chicago-based Lind Waldock.*

We're a futures commission merchant—an FCM. That's like a broker in the securities industry. We trade on behalf of CTAs and take a commission. We were one of the first futures brokers to run a discount operation. We're sort of like Charles Schwab in that regard. Also, many FCMs trade for their own account as well as for clients, but we're a pure agency broker, which makes some of our clients more comfortable.

The managed futures business has been growing because in the early 1990s alternative investments yielded minuscule returns. Now, people are willing to take a little more risk based on track records of CTAs who have managed money for many years. Also, commodities are much more regulated than they used to be, and they're basically their own asset class by now. Before you would mention porkbellies, and people thought that's like going to Las Vegas. They didn't consider futures in the same league with stocks and bonds. Now they are. You've seen allocations by major pension funds to commodities. The state of Virginia decided to allocate some of its pension fund to CTAs in the late 1980s. That was a watershed. Since then, other pension plans have allocated funds for futures.

We have a public that's much more educated about investing—another reason that managed futures investing is growing. And there are more sophisticated trading advisers as well with the onslaught of data feeds and all the information available. The computer has been a major part of this phenomenal growth.

————————◆————————

## FUTURES AND REFLATION

### "It's always hard to predict rates."

JOHN FRAWLEY *runs what is perhaps the largest group of managed futures funds in the United States for Merrill Lynch.*

It's always hard to predict rates. But if the next major move is up, then to participate in that move you sell bonds short because bond prices will go down as inflation heats up. As professional managers, we would have a portion of a fund participating through futures contracts on the short side of an interest rate move. Futures trading allows you to sell bonds short and to sell stock short as well.

But in an inflationary or deflationary environment, you would want to do more than sell bonds or stock short. You would want to be invested in commodities as well as financials. The five sectors we trade are financials, currencies, metals, energy and agriculture. If in an inflationary period, it would be reasonable to think metals values might go up—and a way to participate in that movement is to invest in futures contract. But the question is, How do you access the markets? An individual investor who wants to participate in these markets needs a number of things he probably doesn't have. Investors need a great deal of assets because these are high-risk transactions. As with any other kind of investment I would prefer to have diversification.

Managed futures can avail a person of the ability to invest in a fund having multiple managers using multiple strategies in multiple markets. All of our managers are selected from the outside. It's our job to find the best managers we can. We use about 30 different advisers. We have about 60 percent invested with systematic trend followers and the other 40 percent with discretionary traders. A pure discretionary trader weighs the fundamentals of the market as to when to buy and sell a contract. Discretionary traders operate more on feel than trend followers do, and the two types of investing tend not to be correlated. As people become more sophisticated in the management of their own assets, there is increasing need to understand diversification and act on its principles. That's at the heart of it.

———————◆———————

## INDEX INVESTING

*"I don't see why the individual investor shouldn't be able to purchase exposure to a commodities index on a securities exchange or through a mutual fund."*

GREGORY OBERHOLTZER *is managing director of Intermarket Management, one of a handful of firms using derivatives to customize unique commodity investments.*

Our business is selling commodity hedges mostly to pension plans. Unfortunately, an investment in a commodities index is not practical for most individual investors at this time.

The first commodity-linked product was initiated in the Civil War. That was a cotton bond in which cotton was used as collateral for a war bond in the South. Over the last several years we've seen more and more commodity-linked debt deals issued as a way of raising capital. The Wall Street firms of Salomon Brothers and Goldman Sachs have done these deals.

What we're doing is offering clients a commodities linkage through securitization. We made a deal whereby the Union Bank of Switzerland (UBS) issues a note to our clients. It works like this. First, the client lends money to UBS. Then UBS says "I will return this money to you at a certain time, and I will give you back principal and interest that is pegged to a commodity index."

The client is not necessarily guaranteed the principal or interest. But if the index goes up a great deal, the client can make a very competitive return. Occasionally, we'll sell these notes to high-net-worth individuals.

You can see this is a complex transaction. Now investors can purchase exposure to a commodity index on a listed futures exchange, but it's an expensive way for a small investor to invest passively.

———————◆———————

## THE FUTURE OF FUTURES

*"As the money gets bigger, the industry is under pressure to reduce fees."*

CHUCK EPSTEIN, *a former marketing executive for the New York Futures Exchange, runs a consulting service, Ravinia Associates. He is author of* Managed Futures in the Institutional Portfolio *(1992) and* Handbook of Corporate Earnings *(1994).*

Futures managers offer a wide variety of investments at different cost structures that still suffer from high loads and little transferability. Merrill Lynch and a few others are starting to create funds whereby you can transfer back and forth between managed futures. As the industry matures, there may start to be a greater variety of investment strategies and fee structures offered. Trend followers even now have a lot of different options. They can override their computerized strategies, follow discretionary trend systems, or be intuitive.

The managed futures business didn't take off until about five years ago. The propellant was institutional recognition—the recognition that futures may have a role in an institutional portfolio. In the 1970s, the state of Alaska bought a ton of gold, real estate funds, forests, and other tangible assets. But with futures you don't need to do that. These tangible products can be securitized. Now the cost structures are coming down, portfolio diversification is a main attraction, and people are getting interested.

There is a difference between managed futures and mutual funds. The key factor that helped mutual funds was the creation of the money market fund that people used as a checking account when they didn't want to be invested. The managed futures industry doesn't have this feature, and the way it's organized, it can't. Managed futures provide either a high return or portfolio diversification.

But managed futures may still play a bigger role in the investment industry, even though the industry is under pressure at the moment because of a variety of trading and fundamental factors. As the money gets bigger, the industry is under pressure to reduce fees and offer access to both the cash and futures market. The industry also is providing new trading systems. Globex, the electronic trading system, is an after-hours futures trading network initially designed to trade Eurodollars and foreign currencies. But it's had a rough time with industry acceptance because the traders on the floor don't want electronic trading. The real problem with the futures industry—like stock trading at the Big Board—is that members are in charge of the industry's evolution. They're in charge because the regulations have been built around them. In New York, the chairman of the stock exchanges serves at the pleasure of the Big Board's specialists. Since the Big Board is a self-regulatory organization, supervised by the SEC but with tremendous power within the industry, the stock industry's setup is pretty much controlled by a hundred Big Board specialists. That's why electronic exchanges are having such a hard time gaining ground in both New York and Chicago. Electronic exchanges are cost-effective and efficient—they tend to close the spread. There's no percentage in efficient markets. Professional traders want inefficient markets, where most of the order flow is dumb or moves on old news.

The industry has problems, but that doesn't mean that anybody is going to rock the boat too much. In Chicago, investigations are usually threatened around election time, and they usually threaten to tax futures. I remember once I checked on the bill that was introduced by then-Mayor Jane Byrne of Chicago to impose a city transaction tax on the futures exchanges. It was a verbatim introduction of a previous bill, introduced by Mayor Richard J. Daley, that was designed to tax the exchanges. Byrne's bill even included a typo that slipped through in the bill some four years earlier. Of course the bill was withdrawn after the election, but I'm sure by then the exchanges ponied up plenty of contributions for the incumbent. That's why it was introduced in the first place.

# WHAT I LEARNED

In my interviews with Hot Money pros, it became clear that the first breath of competition is nipping at futures fees despite the clubby nature of this Chicago-based industry. Of course, as Hot Money author Chuck Epstein observes, plenty of problems remain in the futures industry. Just like the larger securities industry, the futures industry continues to be tied to physical exchanges, with dealers and traders controlling the order flow. In fact, the futures industry's organization mimics the worst features of the stock trading industry: the insularity of the players and the dominance of certain large and manipulative trading entities. The setup, as we've observed, is far more sympathetic to large players than to small.

The tight relationship between top industry executives and CFTC regulators virtually guarantees that the system will remain at least a somewhat closed loop until competition, in the form of electronic trading (between investors, not dealers), forces it open. This is especially evident in the ongoing difficulties that the international electronic Globex futures market has caused the industry.

It's Epstein's opinion—one I share—that the apparent failure of Globex may be a good thing since it will give other, more democratic systems time to emerge—if regulators will let them. The rise of true electronic trading systems run by third-party entrepreneurs rather than dealers or institutions, and offering a more unrestricted access to a broad spectrum of players and market makers is the hope of the future for securities trading of all kinds.

Unfortunately, as we've seen, central bankers, regulators, and industry players have a vested interest in resisting easily accessed electronic nets because unrestricted liquidity by definition—flowing from net to net—is harder to organize and control. Moneyed interests suffer when they can no longer stand between the customer and the market. Such interests will inevitably exclaim that restricted access to markets is necessary because brokers must be creditworthy and customers may not be. But this is like saying that customers may not buy cars, clothes, or washing machines without the help of a financial intermediary to guarantee creditworthiness. It is perfectly possible in the future that organizations will insure buyers and sellers who wish to participate in electronic trading. Such investors, through a password or some other device, would be allowed on the network. Chances are such individuals would often not be part-time investors but full-time professionals or dedicated day traders. The politics and bid-rigging that are part of physical exchanges like the Merc and the Chicago Board of Trade—politics that even the most successful Hot Money traders like Mark Ritchie openly mourn—would be reduced.

If the United States is eventually to go through a relatively prolonged reflation, as it will sooner or later, then the domestic futures industry has an exceptional opportunity to garner customers and profits. While most futures traders are trend followers (a strategy developed from gaming theory) and therefore cannot make money in a flat market, it is also true that new forms of futures trading for investors could minimize some of the more aggressive kinds of trading. If indexed investing strategies could be adopted by managed futures, it is likely that the popularity of the product would increase. What is also likely is that in a reflation, given the current computerized environment, investors will see more and more securitization of hard assets. As Gregory Oberholtzer points out, this is already happening for institutional investors who can buy a security priced off a commodities basket. But he admits he doesn't have much comfort to offer individual investors at the moment who want the countercyclical diversification that commodities seem to offer. Of course investors can purchase individual commodities, but this strategy takes time and money. Additionally, a large shakeout in the market can leave the investor vulnerable to margin calls.

There are also several commodity indexes investors can trade, but the investor can either buy these indexes on margin, in which case he can lose his money in a hurry (since he's buying with tremendous leverage), or he can buy the index "unmargined" which can easily cost him over $100,000, depending on where the price of the underlying commodities basket is at the time of purchase.

As I write, Oberholtzer's firm is working on a way to list warrants on securities exchanges that would allow individual customers to purchase exposure to the commodity index without having to spend upwards of $100,000. Interestingly, Oberholtzer wants to list his product on either the American or Philadelphia stock exchanges.

This points out the dilemma of the futures industry: Having pioneered large scale derivatives trading of securities, the industry has not yet succeeded in making those same derivatives available in any meaningful way to the smaller investor.

The fact remains, a simple commodity index purchase isn't feasible for the individual investor; neither is there any pure mutual fund an investor can buy that would provide this exposure. That something so simple as a commodity index fund is not commonly available at this time is a question for Congress, regulators and securities industry execs to answer as best they can.

# INVESTMENT SUMMARY
◆
## HOT MONEY: DIFFICULTIES OF DIVERSIFYING

◆ Diversification is a necessary part of a modern investor's portfolio, and in fiat money's deflation-reflation cycle, investors must look to purchase either tangible assets or Hot

Money securitized assets. The problem with purchasing tangible assets is that it's difficult to purchase enough different classes to be properly diversified. It may be better to purchase at least some assets through futures funds. The goal here is to find a reputable fund that will invest responsibly.

♦ Diversification is achievable within tangible assets. Hot Money funds especially use a broad array of instruments. But often Hot Money is driven by similar trend-oriented investment strategies, which can detract from return. Especially in so-called trendless markets, Hot Money results can lag.

♦ International diversification encompasses more than asset class diversity, but Hot Money investing, often requiring intensive trading, is less diversified when it comes to strategies.

## WHAT THE INVESTOR CAN DO

♦ To ensure maximum equity diversification, seek out tangible investments, offshore if possible, to avoid taxes.

♦ Try to find reputable managed futures efforts for additional diversification. Such funds or pools with the ability to run on the long and short side of the market in a variety of investments offer investors the maximum flexibility in an unstable rate environment.

♦ Be aware of securitized hard-asset investments that will probably appear in a reflationary environment. Such securitized instruments will probably be even more volatile than ordinary futures instruments, though at the beginning of the trend they may offer investors good opportunities.

## HOT MONEY PROBLEMS THAT REMAIN

♦ Hot Money is a growing investment alternative, but it is
a new one in an industry that suffers from a difficult reputation. Investors should try to ensure they're dealing with a
reputable agent.

♦ Hot Money is leverage-intensive since most Hot Money
traders will avail themselves of contracts that allow them
to use significant leverage. Such leverage can lead to quick,
large losses.

♦ Hot Money remains hostage to an industry that is still
largely built around physical pit trading, domestically at
least. This tends to generate an inbred trading environment
in which professional insiders gain an edge over everyone
else, including customers. Until the commodities industry,
including its regulators, comes to terms with its electronic
future, the industry's potential will remain largely un-
tapped, its promise constrained and its profitability diminished.

## CHAPTER SIX

# CONSULTANTS AND CONCLUSIONS

◆

## Planners, Timers, and Financial Futurists

Marketshock comes in many guises. Even the newest growth has roots in age-old regulatory systems and physical-exchange structures. The idea that stock trading is the only healthy form of capital raising, that stocks can be traded only on a physical-exchange floor under the watchful eyes of appropriate regulators, that futures and derivatives are an unhealthy form of speculation: such arguments can be extended indefinitely until they take on a Luddite flavor. One expects to read about top financial leaders who have snapped finally, flailing about with sledgehammers in a vain attempt to smash the technology that is replacing them. In fact this did happen back in the 1970s when some New York Stock Exchange (NYSE) floor members crept onto the Big Board's trading deck and smashed computer screens with axes.

If only government were able to restrain itself from deficit spending, if only central bankers were truly not responsive to their federal masters. Alas, government can't maintain self-control for any length of time, and central banks are more responsive to political concerns than bankers like to admit. The idea of a truly independent central banking system is probably fiction, but it is one that will become more destructive as Europe moves toward centralization and banking explanations become more convoluted and shrill.

Government interference with free markets is like a velvet sledgehammer. The average citizen is unaware of the hidden power until the market has jumped around with such massive force that his or her life savings are in jeopardy. In a fiat-money system, currency is often so unstable that the average investor, confused about what is going on, needs the harbor of increasingly complex government-authorized pension and 401(k) plans. But such government-run plans may eventually lead to more problems. For instance, these enormous capital pools need to be carefully watched over. Government, having set the problems in motion through fiat money, compounds the problem by creating complex savings structures that need constant supervision. The pattern is the same in every instance, from the savings and loan (S&L) crisis to junk bonds to the merger and acquisition madness, and on and on. Bigness is not by itself something that markets and democracies ought to fear, but bigness mandated by government, supported by regulation and advanced by federally granted monopolies is another matter.

This last chapter is, like the first, subdivided in several ways. The first interviews deal with professional consultants, brokers, and planners who can give small but savvy investors additional financial guidance. Next come the insiders who deal with asset allocation and timing approaches. While it is true that many allocaters tend to recommend mostly combinations of securitized instruments such as stocks and bonds, the information they use and the techniques they apply are useful to the investor interested in the larger issue of business-cycle macromarket investing. Finally, we speak to the big-picture insiders who are concerned with how the financial industry is unfolding worldwide. Here's a summary:

*Planners and Brokers.* Investors who have read this far may want to find some professional help when choosing securitized and tangible assets to invest in. In my previous book, *Rebuilding Wall Street*, I pointed out how difficult it was to trust securities salesmen like brokers, who derived a commission from peddling product. At the time I suggested that a fee-based arrangement was preferable to commissions and would diminish abuses. It so happens there is a movement on Wall Street, and among independent brokers as well who work with smaller firms, to offer customers fee-based financial advice. In truth, pressures to sell product will probably never be much diminished, but the investor might do worse than seek out some of these new-style planners and brokers.

*Timers and Allocators.* Money pros who understand business cycles can provide a resource for investors interested in fundamental—business-cycle—allocation. The investor should keep in mind that what we are calling macromarket allocation doesn't necessarily have a great deal to do with moving in and out of the stock market. On the contrary, the investor's efforts should be oriented toward a broad strategy of diversification. An internationally diversified investor can use an understanding of economic cycles to support and enhance diversification strategies.

*Conclusions.* This final section deals with suggestions to rationalize securities regulation in the information age. This is another part of the education that informed investors should undertake. In a changing financial environment, investors who wish to protect themselves need to understand what the problems are, as well as their potential solutions. The September 1993 issue of *Economist* had an excellent article on regulation in the new financial era. The author, Rupert Pennant-Rea, former editor of the *Economist* and now governor of the Bank of England, wrote about settlement and disintermediation as well as the principles of global securities supervision: "The biggest danger to 21st-Century world finance may well be an excess of official zeal. In their search for tidiness and comprehensiveness, governments may lay down rules for financial institutions that are far too restrictive for economic health."

Pennant-Rea says settlement issues are some of the more important elements that need rationalizing in tomorrow's world of electronic finance. He also makes the point that issues having to do with large-scale defaults are necessarily mitigated when international finance is conducted by the world's biggest and presumably most knowledgeable players. In this opinion, he is joined by financial futurist Peter Schwartz, who thinks that what may emerge worldwide over the next decade or two is some kind of two-tier market. This would consist of a relatively unregulated group of perhaps 100 to 1,000 transition or global companies involved in international trading and underwriting evolving on top of a regionalized market structure. In such an environment, it's possible that the biggest players would serve as their own regulatory agents and provide their own free-floating exchange nets. Consumers investing through such entities would receive the protection not of a regulatory authority but of the agent itself.

As Pennant-Rea points out, finance is about risk, and there are no ways of making a risky business risk-free. But if domestic and international regulators will take a step back from rulemaking and, at least as a first step, help business organize its transborder finances more rationally through electronic exchange mechanisms, then 21st-Century finance may be healthier and happier than the financial industry of the recent past.

# PLANNERS AND BROKERS

◆

## INVESTMENT SUMMARY

*"In a fiat-money environment you are bled
to death drop by drop. What's a drop of
blood every single day?"*

KENNETH TARR *is the former head of U.S. asset management for
Crédit Suisse, one of the world's largest and most powerful banks.*

Anyone today who thinks that an event which has an effect on
our economy is not going to have an impact on South America
or Europe is out of touch with the realities of the marketplace.
The computer and rapid information dissemination have changed
everything. These changes have also affected the dynamics of the
markets so that they are becoming more highly correlated. It
may not seem so, but in the next financial crisis, all markets
will be affected. Therefore, investors must diversify across asset
classes. The concept—and it's a comforting one—of diversification around the world to reduce risk is something that money
managers love to chant to make their clients feel safe. But during
the 1987 stock market fall, many markets were affected.

The reason to invest outside the United States is to earn more
than the risk-free rate of return. In order to do so, one must
assume more risk. For most investors, developing an investment
plan that really protects against the investment unknowns is like
writing a will. They hate to think of the reason why they need
to do it and do not review it annually. A very simple fail safe
plan divides assets into thirds: a third in equities, a third in
gold, and a third in reserves with rebalancing annually. This
strategy will protect in both a low and high interest rate environment, although you won't be able to buy Trump's former yacht
with it.

Currency, stocks, and bonds are nothing but paper. Their values are based on confidence. When faith and confidence are shaken, you need a real money strategy. I was once quoted as saying that in every generation, there is an event that separates investors from their capital, and we have not seen that event for this generation of investors. The 1987 crash was not it. What will happen when the casino on Wall Street stops its winning streak? At first, there will be 200 people lining up at the Fidelity office on Park Avenue. Then the media will report how thousands are cashing out of their equity mutual funds. Eventually there will be thousands more wanting out.

Remember that basic motivations—faith, fear, and greed— underlie the financial markets and affect it at various times. When rational behavior breaks down, the wave begins and everyone is swept along. It takes on a life of its own. Throughout the early 1990s, money poured into mutual funds. Investors are projecting that their recent past experience will continue indefinitely. This will change and, unfortunately, surprise many.

There are other surprises on the way for investors. The erosion of the purchasing power of the U.S. dollar is happening very slowly. In a fiat-money environment, you are bled to death drop by drop. What is a drop of blood every single day? The erosion is in such a very slow time frame that it is difficult to grasp what is happening. Fiat money is a disease of both democracies and dictatorships. Gold has been a store of value in the past, but who's to say that gold will be a store of value in the future? Salt, for example, was a store of value because it was used to preserve meat. Therefore, even the best investment plan today has to have contingencies for the unknowns. Unfortunately, many investors do not want to endure mediocre returns that hedging for the unknowns sometimes produces.

The world survived 1987, and many went on to make fortunes. The recent investment experience is positive, and investors, even if confused, have been pleased with equities in the early 1990s.

Those who have held gold and reserves are not. Unfortunately, markets do not accommodate the masses, and things will change. Fear will again overpower faith and greed.

HOWARD SILVERMAN (*see page 149*)

I think at the cornerstone of any investment program has to be discipline. This is where most investors fail. Wall Street doesn't help very much because they tend to make investors go to the place where the performance is the most interesting—at the moment. Trees don't grow to the sky, and what's interesting now may not be over the next 10 years. How will inflation have an impact on investors? Doing an option overriding strategy—writing a covered call, a call option against stock you own—protects you on the downside to a limited extent. It's a clever strategy, but you couldn't do it with most mutual funds.

Investing has both a micro- and a macrolevel. On a microbasis, investors certainly have the ability to pick through the universe of mutual funds and buy ones they are the most comfortable with. But on the macrolevel, investors can use assistance. Self-management is time-consuming. That comes back to the investment discipline. That's where value can be added on the part of someone overseeing their portfolios.

It has become easier in the last several years to commit resources to asset classes, and investors may need help with that. We live in a dynamic environment, and a seemingly viable plan can change very quickly based on the asset classes owned. Risk is nothing more than the reasonable assurance of capital over a certain time frame. There's risk in a 20-year bond and there's risk in a 90-day T-bill. The way I see it, money managers from a broad standpoint have always failed to outperform the index.

One way to get around that is to put funds into an outlier strategy—some funds into a relatively risk-diverse, low-overhead portfolio and then 5 percent into riskier assets. Of course, that's not what Wall Street wants to hear. But products coming on line will allow the investor to manage funds. If the investor needs someone to help him understand his own level of comfort, there are brokers and planners who can help. One has to go through the process of referral seeking a broker oriented toward long-term capital gains.

◆

## BULLISH VIEW

### *"I'm personally stressing international investments because so many countries are moving toward capitalism."*

PETER PRENTIS, *a broker and certified financial planner with Prudential Securities, has over $150 million under his control.*

International investing across asset classes is often part of an investor's strategy. But the reality is that you have to start with needs-based financial planning. Most investors need an appropriate allocation among a reserve fund for emergencies, bonds to supply cash flow, and safety and equities for growth.

International exposure can provide important diversification. The U.S. market can often be out of sync with foreign markets. The world economies are certainly tied together, but countries have different cycles depending on their natural resources, labor base, oil base, and other assets. My advice for investors looking at the international arena is to approach it via professional money managers. For many investors, an appropriate vehicle would be an international mutual fund.

Investing is a process of constantly reviewing potential risk and rewards around the world as well as domestically. I'm optimistic about the market in the 1990s. What if I had told you a couple of years ago that you're not going to have the Cold War, that peace is going to break out, that tariffs are coming down, and that many countries would be capitalist?

I'm stressing international investments because so many countries are moving toward capitalism. By 1995, 30 countries will be privatizing their telecommunications industry—and many of these are countries that have not had access to capital for years.

CHARLES FAHY, *a top stockbroker with Oppenheimer & Co., runs close to $200 million.*

You take any amount of time, say equity over the last five years, and you have about an 80 percent chance of your portfolio of stocks doing better than bonds. With a 20-year period you've got a 100 percent chance.

Here's the problem with bonds. You buy a bond at a fixed rate and as soon as inflation kicks in, your rate return erodes. You can't really win with bonds.

When you invest in stocks, you're investing optimistically. You're making a statement that nothing terrible is going to happen to the country or the economy.

I do feel, however, that people should make some allowances for the unexpected. They should have 60 to 90 days of pure cash as well as metals and jewelry—at least 5 percent of net worth.

I think we'll see the market reach 10,000 before the turn of the century. You have to be in stocks to participate in this move. There's just no way around it. Stocks are what is going to make the investor real money in the 1990s.

———◆———

## DEFLATIONARY VIEW

*"You'd be surprised how many people I meet who are thinking of leaving the country."*

MICHAEL MARTIN *is a fee-only financial planner and founder of the*
*planning firm Financial Advantage in Elliot City, Maryland. He's*
*also a former top equities analyst for giant T. Rowe Price mutual funds.*

We call ourselves money managers because we manage clients'
money for a flat fee. We'll figure out what the client's goals are
and then use no-load mutual funds for investment vehicles. That's
new. Computers have allowed funds to reduce operating expenses
so private money managers can charge a competitive fee, even
adding in the ongoing fees of the mutual fund. We think no-
load mutual funds are increasingly the best kind of vehicle for
the average investor. For almost everything except straight fixed-
income investing, I use mutual funds. In Latin America I use
Scudder funds.

By buying companies in parts of the world where the economy
can grow quickly, the investor can gain a considerable advantage
over countries with slower growth patterns. In many countries
there's increased respect for private property, especially in Asia,
and that's a positive sign. Some Asian countries can grow three,
four, or five times our real rate of growth, and people with money
are still calling the shots in those countries.

We're in an income-transfer mode in this country. Canada and
Europe have already got the message you have to go back, but
in emerging countries, the people who are making the policy are
the ones who have the money, so they won't make the kinds of
economic mistakes we have. Democracy has in it the seeds of its
own destruction. The public has figured out it can vote itself
largesse from the public purse, and that will kill the golden
goose. You'd be surprised how many people I meet who are
thinking of leaving the country.

I think some of the layoffs we've seen in the last business
cycles are permanent. It's the beginning of a postindustrial
economy. I even think there's a chance of deflation. I believe

the economy won't boom until the year 2000, and the 1990s will be a decade of low return on capital. In that scenario and if rates keep falling, the best strategy is to invest in long bonds for the appreciation.

If there was a credible momentum to reverse the income-transfer nature of our society, it would be dramatically helpful for the animal spirits of capitalism. The use of credit would start to pick up. But unless something like that happens, I tend to favor fixed-income exposure, but not at the expense of diversification. It is important for people to get some ideas about diversifying their portfolios. And people have to understand basic truths about investing. Try to anticipate what the government is going to do. Understand cause and effect. It's absolutely necessary.

---

## FINANCIAL PLANNING VIEW

### *"The world will not accommodate stupidity in money."*

RICHARD WAGNER *is chairman of the board of one of the nation's top financial planning organizations, the Institute of Certified Financial Planners, and a partner in the planning firm of Sharkey, Howes, Wagner & Javer. Wagner's group is intimately involved in the certification of the expanding planning industry.*

More and more the international financial system is being regulated by speculators. That's a scary thing to say, but it's true. The average investor can try to protect himself by diversifying across asset classes and industry sectors. But who do you go to for advice about how to build a portfolio of funds? Financial planning professionals provide a major source of consulting for the average investor.

When potential clients walk through the door, we introduce them to us, show them a model investment policy and try to find out what they're looking for in a planner. We're sort of like a fund of funds. We're managing the baseball team.

But what we do doesn't have a lot to do with the issue of how we get paid. We happen to be fee-only planners, but I view that as a matter of choice. It's a minor issue. As a planner, I'm tired of having to be apologetic for getting paid. We are going to get paid because we perform a service. People have different ways of getting paid for services. I care only that the people I'm paying keep their promises. Some of the best financial advice I know comes from brokers, some of the worst from fee-only planners.

If I had to decide on a financial planner, it certainly wouldn't be on the method of payment. It would be on personality match, level of trust, type of clients, whether he was a certified financial planner. As planners, I think we have a big job in front of us. We have to deal with the whole issue of financial illiteracy. The world will not accommodate stupidity in money, and the job of the financial planner is to come to grips with those forces. More and more, money dominates as a social lubricant—not class or privilege but money—and I can't envision any other force more important unless we go back to barter. It's not an unmixed blessing. It's a harsh force for people who aren't competent about it—people who aren't capable of making it or managing it. For them, it's a tough life. Those who want to function in this type of environment and are capable of functioning must know how to gain the money management skills they'll need.

My three rules are simple: Save more, spend less and don't do anything stupid. Money is the crucible in which modern people act morally and religiously. That's why people who inherit money so often feel there's a lack of meaning in their life. They're not motivated by what everyone else is.

———————◆———————

## INVESTMENT CONSULTING

### *"We believe informed clients are better consumers."*

EVALYN BRUST *is the executive director of the Denver-based Investment Management Consulting Association (IMCA).*

IMCA was formed in 1985 to educate financial professionals on how to consult with clients about investment choices, including mutual funds and money managers. We have nearly 1,000 members at major brokerage firms, as well as independent consulting companies.

The financial industry has had bad press, and we want to counteract that in a responsible way. We've brought together other professional associations to analyze why the industry has had negative press and to develop a public education campaign. We believe informed clients are better consumers. We've set up a certification course for members—a week-long course, technically and mathematically oriented, taught at Wharton Business School. We've already had 300 members go through the program. In order to stay certified, individuals must maintain an additional 40 hours every two years.

We want to develop additional standards for consultants. We're developing a consultant's responsibility statement that will include standards about reporting on a customer's portfolio and what that report should include. We don't think this business is about selling the hottest stock. We think it's about selecting suitable managers and then adequately monitoring their performance.

# TIMERS AND ALLOCATORS

◆

### 21st CENTURY FUNDAMENTALS

## *"The big Wall Street firms that own those funds don't want us to call the timing."*

COREY COLEHOUR *is president of Society of Asset Allocators and Fund Timers (SAAFTI), which manages some $9 billion in aggregate, and co-owner of Denver-based Schield Management.*

The early 1990s saw a great bull run, but there will be a correction and that's when market timing can shine. Here at Schield we have 5,000 customers, and if they give us a complete bull- and bear-market cycle to perform, the numbers show that our timing strategy will consistently outperform those who just buy and hold.

One out of every four families has mutual funds, but not everyone can hold funds forever. Nobody knows when a family tragedy—a death, loss of job, or divorce—can force you to liquidate, and liquidating in a bear market costs money.

We look at monetary policy to determine broad market trends and then look at the prices of 4,000 stocks. The prices go into the computer, and we get an indication of which way the momentum is headed. We get a buy or sell signal, but our signals don't switch so much, and in fact on average we get in and out of markets only perhaps four times a year.

Our firm has been around for 21 years, and while we probably won't add much value to a portfolio invested in conservative instruments, with the more volatile funds we'll do very well. We'll outperform the buy-and-hold strategy on the volatile funds—growth funds, global funds, and gold funds.

A lot of the criticism of market timing as a strategy comes

from Wall Street. Most of the biggest funds are load funds, and most of the business in those funds comes from brokers and financial services. The big Wall Street firms that own those funds don't want us to call the timing, they may be bullish when we're bearish or vice versa.

Our kind of investing is the investing of the future. I can see the day when we'll advocate switching in and out of stocks, bonds, cash and even futures—commodities and financial futures. That would be a reasonable evolution of what we're doing.

BOB KARGENIAN *is a wirehouse broker with a major retail firm.*

Individual investors probably can do some kind of macro-asset allocation to track cycles in stocks, bonds, commodities, and gold. But in my experience, an investor should try this kind of strategy in tandem with somebody who can impose some discipline on the strategy. You've got to hook up with the right money manager or planner. My experience is that many people in this business don't have a working knowledge of markets and cycles. I'm self-taught from reading and studying books. I've paid some painful dues.

I pay close attention to monetary policy as well as to moving averages and price data. The idea is to find out what people are doing in the market and which moves signal a fundamental change in economic climate. It takes a lot of discipline. Not everyone can do it.

CHARLES MIZRAHI *and his brother, Gary, are developing software to manage funds for institutional and retail clients.*

These days the number of funds outnumber the number of stocks, so there has to be a shakeout. I used to be a floor trader at the New York Futures Exchange. There were a handful of funds available. But now turn on the radio, and you'll hear what the

London market did, what Paris did, what gold did, and where the long bond is. We're definitely living in a global village, and investors should take it into account. If a person sneezes in the global village, we can all catch a cold. In 1992 the currency crash hurt our stock market and made interest rates move all over the place. The fact that you're refinancing your mortgage has a lot to do with what's happening in Europe.

People should try to buy a number of different instruments, including international funds. But what does it tell me when global markets are in upsurges? It tells me that markets are going to work in tandem. Market timing and asset allocation are gaining among money managers and among financial planners because these strategies are gaining popularity among investors.

# CONCLUSIONS
◆

## DOMESTIC FINANCE

*"The politics of regulation go back to
Andrew Jackson, and it's extraordinarily
bad politics. The United States was
founded by debtors who distrusted centers
of financial power."*

WILLIAM SIHLER, *professor at the Darden Graduate School of Business, University of Virginia, coauthored an insightful look at the financial industry,* The Troubled Money Business.

Once we had a financial system in which everything fit together and everything had an assigned role. S&Ls provided loans for housing; commercial banks were in the consumer lending business and loaned money to private business; investment banks raised cash from the public for investment in private and public enterprises; insurers took in public money and guaranteed a return in case of trouble.

Now efforts to regulate our current system the way we regulated the previous system are causing the problems. We're trying to mandate certain requirements for our banks that make them less competitive in the marketplace. As a result, they can't attract the capital they need to survive.

S&Ls are dead. The fundamental flaw of borrowing short and lending long killed them. Commercial banks and insurance companies are struggling. In fact, these two kinds of financial enterprises are becoming more alike. Insurance companies are actually a form of a bank, except that commercial banks have traditionally taken shorter risks, insurers the longer. Insurance customers tend to "deposit" money for the long term; insurers take in deposits in the form of premiums and then sometimes, years later, pay them back out.

Now insurance companies are taking in deposits for shorter periods of time. Insurers are offering more and more group policies as opposed to traditional whole life policies. A group policy is a more unstable funding source because the company purchasing the group policy might take its business elsewhere next year. Whole life customers tend to be with an insurer for a much longer period. Insurance companies now have the same kind of uncertainties as commercial banks, except they have no Federal Reserve window—no government lender of last resort—the way the commercial banks do. Additionally, insurance companies are struggling because of new societal ills that they are expected to insure but for which their policies and current structure are unsuited. This is leading to new, and sometimes smaller, companies with more flexible policies aimed at fewer individuals in some cases. Insurers, commercial banks, and S&Ls have a less stable base of investors. Once commercial banks took almost no risk at all. They funded seasonal inventory and receivables; the customer sold the goods and paid the bank back. Later, banks took the daring step of making term loans—longer loans not paid down by the liquidation of assets but through a portion of earnings. Insurers handled the longest risk of all, since life insurance policies might be paid out only decades after the initial deposits were made.

Now the most stable funding sources belong to mutual funds and pension funds, especially pension plans. These plans have the most stable funding of all since they don't have to pay investors back at all short of death or retirement, and investors are barred from removing their assets. That's a financial intermediary with a long time horizon.

But mutual funds are attracting a good deal of relatively stable investment as well. Demand money is moving into money market funds offered by mutual funds. These funds have no requirement for capital because all their funds are counted as equity. A mutual fund company like Fidelity can reinvest its depositors' money just the way a bank can, but it has no community obligations to consider, no risky loans to make out of a sense of social conscience. Additionally, a firm like Fidelity doesn't have to pay for banking insurance or carry a certain mandated percentage of assets in cash to ensure solvency. Because of these requirements, a bank's cost of capital is higher than a mutual fund's. Government has even prohibited banks from paying market rates of interest on their deposits. In the case of money market accounts at banks, holders can't make more than three withdrawals per month. Consumer demand moves to the more flexible funds, the mutual funds.

There's an old saying, "Capital, like liberty, does not last long where it is not valued." Capital tends to flow where it is respected. In the Great Depression, government and the Fed did all the wrong things. They didn't respect capital, and they aggravated what was already wrong; they raised taxes and embargoed trade. People don't understand that we already had a highly regulated financial system before the 1930s. The politics of regulation go back to Andrew Jackson, and it's extraordinarily bad politics. The United States was founded by debtors who distrusted centers of financial power. Andrew Jackson disbanded the Second National Bank of the United States in 1833. That left banks in individual states. Instead of a federal banking system, we had a state and even a city banking system. Every region wanted its own bank—a money center that could attract the deposits of wealthy people and lend money to build up business. It was a states' rights issue to some degree.

The result was that when the Great Depression came, all these little state and city banks were vulnerable to collapse. Europe didn't have as much of a problem because its banks were bigger. It didn't distrust size so much. Of course, its banks are too big, and there is no competition, but if the banks are too small, you also have problems. In this country, our banks were too small because of our regulatory bias. When the depression came along, all the little state banks started going under. So we regulated more, and that got us to where we are today. Now we have a skewed playing field where banks can't compete. We can keep regulating, but ultimately the consumer will pay the bill. The market is going to evolve anyway. Basically consumers go where they're respected. Money moves. You can't keep it in one place.

Regulators should get out of the way where they can and try to strengthen all market participants. It does no one a service to let insurers and commercial banks go the way of the S&Ls. Further consolidation and more efficient use of capital is what our system needs right now. Our commercial banks especially should be allowed to compete on an equal playing field with our securities firms.

———————◆———————

## INTERNATIONAL FINANCE

### *"A place where consenting adults can have safe sex cheaply."*

PETER SCHWARTZ, *president of Global Business Network, is a futurist and business strategist. His current research encompasses energy resources and the environment, information technology, telecommunications, finance, and entertainment.*

In the 1980s, the scale and scope of the securities industry changed dramatically, but there was a fundamental misconception about the permanence of those changes. It reminded me of what happened in the oil business in the 1970s. Oil companies thought oil prices would keep going up; instead they went down. The securities industry planned for a strong growth scenario that went along as predicted for a while and then went off the tracks.

I don't think the executives in the securities industry or its market regulators are willfully blind to the evolution of the marketplace. It's not the guild's blindly protecting its past; rather, the regulators believe the system they have created is actually superior to what's coming. That's why you get plausible arguments about the virtues of the system in place, the virtues of the physical exchange, or the specialist system. That kind of belief makes things even more dangerous and far more difficult.

The danger is that this blindness, this belief in the perfectibility of our current domestic system, will retard the evolution of our financial markets in the international arena. Regulatory obstruction can retard capital flows; money and jobs will go elsewhere. In the meantime our markets will behave worse and worse. We'll lose efficiency in our own capital-raising mechanism at the same time that we'll lose some access to the new systems that are being created internationally.

A couple of things are quite fundamental in shaping the future of the markets. The first is the increasing rapidity and size of capital flows; the second is the ability to integrate and operate our evolving automated markets; and the third is the eventual stratification of the marketplace. When I was advising the London Stock Exchange, after the Big Bang, I spoke at length with an American securities executive running an overseas subsidiary. He told me, "What we want is a place of our own where consenting adults can have safe sex cheaply." What he was trying to say was that the rules for adults—the world's largest corporations, banks, and money managers—should be different from the rules for the small investor with $50 to invest in IBM. That's starting to be the case anyway. The bulk of international global trading is inefficient and unobserved, and it ripples into our domestic market in ways we often choose to deny. What we're going to get, probably in a piecemeal fashion, is a market for consenting adults with more than $100 million to invest, who have the sophistication and systems to trade in the global arena. These adult players will trade in an environment with a minimum of rules where the biggest risks are counterparty risks: Can I trust the guy on the other side to honor his commitment?

This market will seek out—and demand from international regulators—capital adequacy requirements. Trading rules, the rules of fair practice, the Glass-Steagall legislation, the host of regulations enacted in this country over the last 50 years will probably be irrelevant in the global trading arena. In addition to capital adequacy, global traders will be interested in ensuring they are trading at the lowest possible cost. Efficient, automated systems for executing and settling the trade will be of high value to them. They won't wish to be constrained by boundaries. They'll want efficiency—a minimum of rules and a maximum of efficiency.

All this has tremendous implications. For one thing, we'll have to stop thinking of companies as domestic or foreign. When most of a company's stock is owned by investors outside this country, how can that company be defined as American? Additionally, we're not going to have the control over the international arena that we're used to having over our domestic economy. Inevitably, we'll have an internationally managed marketplace, probably managed by some subset of American, German, English, and Japanese regulators. The French want in too, but they're probably not going to be a factor.

The closest analogy I could probably make is to the unregulated foreign currency market, where large institutions trade among themselves without regulations or publicity. The critical issue is how this new structure will be regulated. I think that the industry's International Organization of Securities Commissions (IOSCO), will empower a standing committee to put together the rules and regulations necessary to make a true international trading area practical. This committee would discuss capital adequacy and what can be counted as capital. It would be a voluntary system, of course. The worst that could happen would be that the countries could boycott other countries that refused to accept or follow the guidelines.

But this new trading environment will probably look radically different from the one we now accept as standard. With true automated systems functioning in a professional environment and run by professional traders, there won't be a lot of the market crimes we now pay attention to. Insider trading, parking stock, and other kinds of market manipulations will be detectable to sophisticated traders. And if they are not detectable, the market may tend to regulate itself, just the way the exchanges used to do before government got involved to protect small investors. These international players will all know each other. If one of them acts up for too long, the others just won't do business with that firm. It's going to be like a physical exchange was, except on a global scale.

There will be another market, probably not as interesting as this international market that's emerging. That will be a domestic, possibly regionalized, market that will be evident in most countries, including this one.

The international markets will be vastly different from those we are accustomed to domestically. They will trade a variety of customized index instruments, highly hedged, and in many derivatives, equities, and bond markets. The old definitions of what constitutes a stock, a bond, or a future will fade, probably along with definitions of what makes up a bank, or a money manager versus a Wall Street firm, or a futures or commodities firm. A lot of these definitions we're used to in this country were imposed by regulations that won't exist in the international arena. But the domestic market will be more familiar. There will probably be physical exchanges—at least at first—electronic communications, and eventually even domestic markets will begin to take on some of the flavor of the international marketplace. But the exchange will be slower, and, depending on the liquidity of the domestic market, investors may find it less risky to invest there. The international market will certainly be a riskier market. One of the troubles we have with markets is that we don't want anybody to lose. But it's the nature of markets that there is loss. Investors with a higher tolerance for risk will probably be able to access the international market through mutual funds. Of course, that will entail changes in the way we regulate mutual funds and what we allow our small investors to invest in. But there is no reason why we shouldn't allow citizens to invest in a global economy.

The process is very similar to what this country went through in the late 1800s when we finally began to establish a true national economy. The way we did business changed. Our systems changed, and so did our regulations. These changes will probably be good for the world. Efficient Third World companies will attract surges of capital from huge private entities instead of depending on handouts from world organizations. The market itself will decide which countries are more efficient and where capital should flow. The risk is that we won't move fast enough in this country. If we don't, if we restrain our banks and corporations, they won't take part so fully. Our own access to capital will diminish. In this country, we'll continue to see great pressure on our domestic exchanges and firms as we strain to make them international players without giving them the regulatory power to compete. We have to recognize the future and let it come. That takes courage and foresight and the will to compete.

# WHAT I LEARNED

When I began this book I was already certain, based on previous research, that financial industry regulations needed changing. Now, at the end of this project, I find my initial certainty in no way shaken. My concerns, as well as my conclusions, have been buttressed by numerous insiders, and I've shared that information, in condensed form, with readers of this book. Kenneth Tarr, Howard Silverman, Michael Martin—all these insiders interviewed for this concluding chapter have deep concerns about the way our financial system is headed. The Darden School's William Sihler and futurist Peter Schwartz, both of whom I interviewed for my first book, have fascinating insights into some of the difficulties of our troubled money business and where it's headed. After talking to these insiders, I feel more strongly than ever that the informed investor must understand the truth about the society in which he or she lives and works, invests, and saves.

Certainly the investor who has read this far should understand more about the way the financial industry interacts with consumers. He should understand—courtesy of Walter Wriston and

John Loofbourrow—more about how computers have affected the financial industry and how the computerization of finance has affected the instruments people invest in and the strategies they use. What hasn't changed so much, as Robert Schwartz and Gregg Kipnis pointed out in Chapter One, is the way the instruments are actually traded and the way the industry in both this country and overseas is organized. A securities industry divided into a buy side and a sell side where order flow moves only rigidly through dealers onto physical exchange trading floors is an industry that will be increasingly subject to structural marketshock.

It may also be true, as financial observer Paul Gibson writes at the beginning of this book, that investors can do nothing to protect themselves from marketshock. Yet they can certainly take some action.

First, they can seek to understand financial markets and business cycles and where our financial system, worldwide, is headed. They can seek out funds in which to invest, bearing in mind the current stage of the business cycle and the nature of the fund or manager with whom they are investing—Big Money, New Money, or Hot Money. Finally, they can learn to monitor their portfolios with or without the help of a broker or planner to ensure that they move at least some funds from asset class to asset class, region to region, and even strategy to strategy, depending on reflationary or deflationary trends.

I've thought of including in the back of this book an actual model allocation of stocks, bonds, commodities, metals, real estate and other assets to show investors how to best diversify in any given business cycle. I decided not to do this because each investor must discover for himself what strategies and allocations he is comfortable with. There are those authors who, throughout their book or at its end, present the investor with this kind of approach. Top business writer Douglas Casey is one such author.

In *Crisis Investing for the Rest of the 1990s* (Birch Lane Press,

1993) Casey presents a Permanent Portfolio that the investor can place funds in that he "must preserve for the future." Such a portfolio, writes Casey, includes gold (20 percent), silver (5 percent), Swiss franc assets (10 percent), real estate/resource stocks (15 percent), U.S. stocks (15 percent) and Treasurys (35 percent).

The above listed allocation is certainly diversified conservatively. Those who are optimistic about our global and domestic financial future would probably suggest a more aggressive equity allocation. Broker Charles Fahy, for instance, is especially vehement on this point. Fahy's idea is that an investor puts money in high-performing stocks (picked by fund pros) and leaves that money there for 20 or 30 years. Of course this is the same wisdom propounded by many of our major business magazines. It should be obvious to anyone who has read this far that I disagree with the passive nature of this strategy. In fact, my insiders have confirmed my initial presumption—that informed investors, practicing macromarket business-cycle asset allocation, worldwide, can both increase returns and decrease risk. (And a fiat-money environment is by definition risky.) Nonetheless, within the larger diversified portfolio, investors more concerned with generating return than conserving capital ought to at least consider some of the ground rules that money pros like Fahy recommend.

Fahy points out that over the long term stocks, especially so-called "growth" stocks—those stocks of promising companies, often with smaller capitalization—have dramatically outperformed bonds and other kinds of asset classes. Fahy would stop here, suggesting a large allocation in growth stocks as well as larger cap stocks along with a very modest investment in tangible commodities (5 percent) and cash on hand for three or four months.

I believe the informed—but aggressive—investor can improve on Fahy's schematic by allocation that would reshuffle at least some equity based on the business cycle. Certainly a savvy investor would not have wanted to be fully invested in stocks during the 1970s. Judicious investments in commodities, especially in gold and real estate, would have certainly have helped raise an individual's net worth during that volatile time period. And in 1987, an investor who anticipated a stock crash because of an earlier bond crash might have saved himself considerable equity depreciation by kicking additional funds over to metals and other commodities which tend to rise in times of economic turmoil. And when it became clear that interest rates were on their way down throughout the early 1990s, an investor might well have upped his fixed-income exposure since bonds appreciate as rates fall.

None of this is to say that the investor should ever abandon equity while making macro portfolio adjustments. But even if an investor wishes to let 70 percent or 80 percent of his or her funds ride in steady-state equity—through private managers or mutual funds—there is no reason why the other 20 percent or 30 percent could not be re-allocated from time to time as circumstances dictated. And within the equity allocation itself, the savvy investor could easily adjust his portfolio, moving some cash from, say, large- to small-cap funds as the business cycle turns, since small cap funds tend to do better later on in the business cycle when large-cap gains are mitigated by inflation.

The investor, as this book has urged, might also want to consider allocation across investment strategies as well as asset classes. Before computers, asset allocation was simply a matter of purchasing different kinds of assets. But now, as my insiders have pointed out, there is another kind of allocation emerging which has to do with the kinds of strategies that are employed by money pros. A diversified investor is seeking to gain maximum profit with minimum risk. Allocation across strategy as well as asset class can certainly qualify as a diversification technique if one considers that the goal is to minimize risk while maximizing profit. Even within the rigid parameters of Big Money, SoGen's relatively flexible asset allocation approach differs radically from Vanguard's index fund strategy. An investor with enough money to pursue wide-ranging strategy diversification could do worse for a portion of his portfolio than hire various Big Money, New Money and Hot Money managers—and reallocate according to strategy as well as asset class depending on the business cycle.

In addition to investing in stock indexes through funds like Vanguard, the investor increasingly has options to invest in indexes by buying derivative instruments such as the American Stock Exchange's SPDRS (see chapter three). Eventually, as we have seen, investors will be able to buy commodity indexes as well without fund participation. As time goes on, the investor no doubt will be able to mix and match portions of these exchange-traded index products the way the biggest institutional buyers now blend their indexed investments. Once this occurs, strategy diversification will come into its own alongside asset-class diversification.

I am aware there are other ways to think about investing than through diversification in vehicles and products provided by the larger securities industry. The more pessimistic among us might simply decide to buy real estate and tangible commodities like gold and to stay away from industry-driven investment vehicles altogether. We live in a real world and must make real choices about what to do with the assets we've been able to accumulate.

But investors should do more than just make up their own minds about how they wish to organize their assets to confront the future. Having educated themselves, they should seek to educate others— family, friends, neighbors, acquaintances. In the era of marketshock, institutional and individual investors will have to be increasingly aware of their own financial condition, and as top planner Richard Wagner wisely observes, take responsibility for it. Government-forced savings programs including Social Security are bound to erode in an environment in which government can't control its own spending. Nor are increased programs an answer.

Famous free-market economist Murray Rothbard helped me understand that healthy money is both the yardstick and the currency of democracy. If coin is debased, then Western-style freedoms are debased also. Hungry people are sullen people. Poor people with little left to lose agitate for change with increasing violence. And violent change usually changes little for the better. The wheel turns, and democracy is eroded.

Economic literacy is an antidote to the kinds of repression and hate that sweep the world at all-too-often intervals, and economic literacy is increasingly necessary as our financial systems grow more complex and globalized.

## Last Word—Conclusions

There is no rule that says freedom can't be eroded in this country as it has been elsewhere (and some would say it already has happened here). Economic instability can give birth to hatred and repression anywhere. Financial euphorias are not hypothetical creations; they are as ruinous as earthquakes, as devastating as hurricanes, as formidable as floods. Our regulatory and financial system does too little to address the reality of an unstable, computerized fiat-money environment. In fact, our current fiat-money system certainly encourages financial euphorias—and the manipulations that go hand in hand with them—by making financial regulations even more inflexible and therefore channeling investments into only a few simplistic vehicles. In our financial system, too much power resides in the hands of powerful dealers, who exacerbate what is already bad. As economic cycles approach their peaks, Wall Street's selling fervor kicks into high gear. Aided by physical-exchange systems and a lack of sunshine on the pricing of a variety of instruments, Wall Street peddles extraordinary amounts of flawed instruments at the top of its selling curve.

The financial industry in this country and overseas is centralized and compartmentalized. To counteract the regulatory bias
toward centralization (not to be confused with market-driven
centralization), a new way of looking at regulation is needed—
one that emphasizes creditworthiness over examination of individual frauds and the creation of rational electronic trading systems
rather than the maintenance of outdated exchanges. Good financial regulation is all about safety: monitoring leverage, encouraging fiscal responsibility, rooting out financial crooks who cheat
and steal. Bad regulation interferes with the structure of the
marketplace, gives certain players power that others don't have,
and raises the level of entry for certain parts of the financial
industry until only a powerful, moneyed few can get in and
operate there.

One way to break the mold of the current financial business
would be to introduce more competition into Wall Street. Laws
that fix prices while preventing various segments of the financial
industry from competing with each other should be done away
with as soon as possible. Another way to induce rationality would
be to encourage further sunshine through the various electronic
systems now coming onto the market.

A third way, as I mentioned at the beginning of this book,
would be to get the government out of the business of insuring
private and institutional risk. The less the government is involved
as the insurer of last resort, the less clout the government will
have within the financial industry.

There are two ways of looking at the evolution of the world's
economy. One is to say that the main thrust of free markets
survives and continues to gain, and certainly in the largest historical context this is true. But in another sense the progress of free
markets has been blunted, worldwide, by government control
over the money supply and by the various levels of taxes and
regulations with which markets struggle. It's one thing to police
financial "fraud"—something regulators do only occasionally.

It's another to respond seriously and responsibly to a marketplace that needs guidance rather than rules and creditworthy players rather than arguments about industry privilege.

To say this is not to hold out hope that it will happen in any cohesive or organized fashion. Regulators, bureaucrats and entrenched industry interests are no more likely to give up power voluntarily than any other professional groups. Yet the power of markets moved even the stubborn, communist Soviet Union toward freedom—at least for the moment. And who is to say that power, the most magnificent, merciless and hopeful force that people have ever discovered, will not triumph in a purer form sooner rather than later.

# RULES OF MARKETSHOCK INVESTING
◆
## As Fiat Money Welcomes the Information Age

Depending on their comfort level, investors should:

◆ Attempt to be invested both globally and domestically in a wide array of instruments, markets, regions, strategies and asset classes—including, importantly, physical commodities, real estate and metals.

◆ Take advantage of every kind of money management strategy available to them, depending on income and personal proclivity: Big Money, New Money, and Hot Money. Investors should try to anticipate the kind of environment central bankers and politicians are creating—inflationary or deflationary—and adjust their portfolio accordingly (more tangible assets during inflation, less in a deflation).

◆ Attempt to familiarize themselves with different kinds of hedging strategies and macro asset allocation methodologies.

♦ Familiarize themselves with the rules and regulations governing the various funds and instruments in which they wish to invest, as well as with the various economic theories that are often used by regulators and the financial industry to confuse investors.

## INTERNATIONAL DIVERSIFICATION: RED FLAGS

Investors should:

♦ Understand the appreciation of investments in developing countries will be inversely proportional to the rapidity of the drop during a marketshock.

♦ Realize that foreign investments may well be considerably less liquid than domestic ones and that markets—especially in rapidly developing countries—may be considerably more concentrated in the hands of a few wealthy individuals.

♦ Beware of financial advisers who promote products from which they receive substantial commissions while declining to recommend less remunerative products.

♦ Avoid Hot Money funds that charge high commissions and high fees for substandard or average performance.

♦ Distrust mutual funds that promise big yields in a low-yield environment. Such yields must be risky bets on interest rates and often result in the investor losing more in the long run than he gains.

♦ Beware of aggressive options strategies that seek to enhance yields in specific stocks.

♦ Proceed cautiously while derivatives mania proceeds apace without proper private-market safeguards worldwide.

♦ Understand that in the United States, years of artificially low rates in the late 1980s and early 1990s will ultimately result in another series of market bubbles, all other things (including the tax code) being equal.

♦ Realize that the continued structure of financial markets at home and abroad, favoring physical exchanges and trading via third parties (intermediation), is a continued invitation to market manipulation, euphorias and crashes.

♦ Try to understand business cycles—at home and abroad—and act accordingly after due consideration and consultation.

# CODA

- Be distrustful of plans floated by federal, state, and local government—with or without private-sector participation—to make your life easier and your retirement safer.
- Have faith in your own skills and your own ability to plan for retirement through the purchase of a varied portfolio of domestic and international investments with or without the guidance of a market pro.
- Watch carefully to see if regulators and Congress recognize any of the realities of fiat money in the information age and allow the financial industry the kind of credible deregulation that would lead to true competition and thoughtful innovation.
- Remember that in a fiat-money and information-rich environment, the only truly successful investors will be economically and computer-literate, industrious and independent of their environment.

Good luck—and good investing.

# INDEX

213